HOW TO PLAN & DESIGN
ADDITIONS

*Created and designed by
the editorial staff of
ORTHO BOOKS*

Project Editor
Kenneth R. Burke

Lead Writers
John R. Musgrave
Fred B. Thompson

Writers
Beverley DeWitt
Christina Nelson

Illustrator
Rik Olson

*Additional
Illustrations*
Ron Hildebrand

Ortho Books

Publisher
Robert L. Iacopi

Production Director
Ernie S. Tasaki

Managing Editors
Anne Coolman
Michael D. Smith
Sally W. Smith

System Manager
Leonard D. Grotta

National Sales Manager
Charles H. Aydelotte

Marketing Specialist
Susan B. Boyle

Operations Coordinator
Georgiann Wright

Office Assistant
Marie Ongsiaco

Senior Technical Analyst
J. A. Crozier, Jr.

Address all inquiries to
Ortho Books
Chevron Chemical Company
Consumer Products Division
Box 5047
San Ramon, CA 94583

Copyright © 1986
Chevron Chemical Company
All rights reserved under international and Pan-American copyright conventions.

    4 5 6 7 8 9
         90 91

ISBN 0-89721-074-3
Library of Congress Catalog Card
Number 86-071057

Chevron Chemical Company
6001 Bollinger Canyon Road, San Ramon, CA 94583

Acknowledgments

Additional Writers
Bruce Finson
Jessie Wood

Consultants
Mark Pechenik
Brett Weinstein

Copy Editor
Jessie Wood

Photo Editor
Cindy Putnam

Layout
Christy Butterfield

Composition and Pagination
Linda Bouchard

Production Artists
Deborah Cowder
Lezlly Freier
Anne Pederson

Proofreader
Andrea Connolly

Indexer
Frances Bowles

Color Separations
Balzer-Shopes

Photography
Laurie A. Black, pages 58: top, 59
David Bohl, Society for the Preservation of New England Antiquities, pages 3: center, 4
Obie G. Bowman, AIA, pages 62–63
Karen Bussolini, ©1981, reprinted by permission of *House Beautiful's Home Remodeling,* ©1982 by The Hearst Corporation, pages 54–55, 86
Centerbrook Architects and Planners, pages 10, 40–41, 42–43
Stephen Cridland, pages 64–67
Hoddick, Berry & Malakoff, page 7: top left
Jerry LeBlond, pages 3: top, 22, 44–45
Stephen Marley Productions, pages 1, 36–39, 52–53
Kit Morris, pages 3: bottom, 34, 46–47, 74
Paul Van Erden Reslink, AIA, pages 7: top right, center, and bottom right; 48–51; 60–61
Durston Saylor, pages 70–73
J. Gregory Tankersley, pages 68–69
Tom Wyatt, pages 56–57, 58: bottom

Architects and Designers
Glenn W. Arbonies, AIA, Centerbrook Architects and Planners, Essex, Conn., pages 40–41
Roderick Ashley, AIA, Portland, Ore., pages 64–67
Eli Sutton, San Rafael, Calif., page 7: top left
Obie G. Bowman, AIA, Sea Ranch, Calif., pages 62–63
Camp Brothers Home Remodeling and Chula Productions, Kitchen Design, San Francisco, Calif., pages 56–59
George Dedekian, AIA, Oakland, Calif., pages 34, 46–47
Robert L. Harper, FAIA, Centerbrook Architects and Planners, Essex, Conn., front cover & pages 10–11, 42–43
Larry Madsen, AIA, Los Altos, Calif., pages 1, 52–53
Paul Pugliese, AIA, Old Greenwich, Conn., pages 22, 44–45, 54–55, 86
Paul Van Erden Reslink, AIA, Stratford, Conn., pages 7: top right, center, and bottom right; 48–51; 60–61
Kathryn E. Schmidt, AIA, Palo Alto, Calif., pages 36–39
Phillip Sides, Sides—McAlpine, Inc., Montgomery, Ala., pages 68–69
Bernard Wharton, AIA, Shope Reno Wharton Associates, Greenwich, Conn., pages 70–71

Special Thanks
Sam Argo, Mortgage Brokers Services, Inc., Seattle, Wash.; Lee Fitch, CHFC, Charles Lee Fitch Ltd., Seattle, Wash.; Rosalie Gorfkle, Interior Designer, Seattle, Wash.; Morley M. Margolis, J and J Remodeling Co., Portland, Ore.; James R. Merrill, Merrill Construction, Inc., Seattle, Wash.; Chuck Moriarty, Moriarty and Matzen, Seattle, Wash.; Tom Steffes, Steffes Design/Construction, Seattle, Wash.; Paul Thienes, AIA, Seattle, Wash.; Robert Zanoni, FAIBD, Robert Zanoni Associates, Seattle, Wash.; Bill Zimmerman, AIA, Seattle, Wash.; Hoddick, Berry & Malakoff, San Rafael, Calif.; Joseph Assif, Waterbury, Conn.; Diane Wieden; Diana DeRagon; Mike and Melissa Haglund; The Jackson Family; The Heydt Family; Mr. and Mrs. James N. Walter; Elinor Ehrman.

Front cover. For more information about this family-room addition to a historic house, see pages 42–43. Photo by Centerbrook Architects and Planners.

Title page. For more information about this addition, see pages 52–53. Photo by Stephen Marley Productions.

Back cover
Top left: Stephen Marley
Top right: Paul Pugliese
Bottom left: Tom Wyatt
Bottom right: Paul Van Erden Reslink, AIA

HOW TO PLAN & DESIGN
ADDITIONS

ADDING ON: AN AMERICAN TRADITION

From our nation's earliest days, Americans have been adding on, enlarging homes, barns, and outbuildings to accommodate their needs. As New England families prospered, their timber-frame homes sported sheds or lean-to additions, or even attached clapboard twins. Mountain dwellers expanded the modest log cabins called cribs or pens by sandwiching them between two sheds or by doubling them up in such colorfully named pairings as dogtrots (two cribs joined by a breezeway) or saddlebags (two cribs flanking a massive central chimney). This tradition is alive, and healthier than ever, among homeowners today.

In these days of urban density and housing shortages, a structurally sound home in an older, close-in suburb is a treasure not lightly parted with. These homes often have generous lots and large rooms, are well-constructed of durable, high-quality materials and boast a distinct architectural style complemented by detailing and decorative elements that newer homes may lack.

If you're lucky enough to own such a home, you may be loath to give it up despite your need for additional space. If you've been feeling cramped, you've probably been thinking about your options. Should you try to rearrange your furniture, perhaps build in some storage space, and make do? Should you sell your home and look for a larger one? Or should you consider expanding the house you already own?

The Tristram Coffin, Jr., house shows clearly that adding on and changing the style to update or "modernize" are traditions deeply rooted in the American past. Eight generations of the Coffin family lived in this house in Newbury, Massachusetts, from 1653 through 1883.

SHOULD YOU ADD ON?

*H*ow do you decide whether adding on makes sense? *There are many factors to consider. Some of those factors, such as the structure and condition of the house and lot, legal restraints like zoning laws, and the economics of adding on, can be weighed and measured. Other factors are very personal: your feelings about the house itself and about the neighborhood, for example. We'll look more closely at these factors in the next chapter.*

Also consider the stresses associated with construction of a major addition. Adding on demands a large commitment of time and money, and it will almost certainly disrupt your daily routines. Exterior walls may have to be removed or broken through; part of the roof may have to be torn off; and there will undoubtedly be plenty of dust, debris, and other inconveniences associated with the demolition that generally precedes adding on. If this kind of major disruption would be hard to handle, buying a new house may be the best way for you and your family to meet your needs for more space.

The gallery section of this book tells the stories of fourteen homeowners across the country who have added much-needed space to their homes. These real-life examples, with their accompanying plans and photographs, will give you an idea of the limitless possibilities for expanding your home.

Options for gaining space

Adding on doesn't necessarily mean constructing a new wing or an entire second story. Before you decide that a major addition is the only answer, let's take a look at a few small options that may meet your needs.

Small changes for a big difference

Sometimes that cramped feeling has more to do with lack of light and ventilation than it does with too little space. The simplest of additions—bump-outs—can solve this problem. Bump-outs are exactly what they sound like—mini-extensions of floors, walls, and roofs that bring a feeling of spaciousness to otherwise confined spaces.

Adding a bay—a windowed extension that begins at the floor of a room—both extends floor space and brings light into a room. A double-story bay can scale the walls of a two-story home. A greenhouse or sun-space addition—really only a large bay—can add substantial space to a room without becoming a room in itself. A bay window and window seat that projects from the structure above ground level does not have to expand floor space to create a feeling of elbow room in cramped second-story quarters.

Adding a gable dormer to a pitched roof can open up a tight second-story room. A shed dormer extending the length of the roof provides even more light and, by improving headroom, increases usable floor space.

Don't overlook "forgotten" space where wings of the original house join each other. A corner enclosure here can sometimes expand two rooms at once.

If your children are doubled up two to a bedroom, or if the living room is always a mess because there's nowhere else for the family to congregate, however, bump-outs won't meet your needs. You'll have to add real floor space to your home.

Substantial add-ons

At first, home design may seem extremely complex—after all, the houses in plan books all look different. When you examine homes more closely, however, mentally stripping them of their porches, roofs, and the decorative elements that give them character, you begin to realize that they have one thing in common. They're all basically arrangements of modular boxes: square and rectangular forms joined in such a way as to please the eye and encourage efficient use of the space they enclose. Enlarging a house simply involves adding one or more modules to the original layout.

Adding on is a bit like a child's game of blocks. If you enjoyed constructing buildings out of blocks and making castles in the sand as a child, you may find planning a major addition the most fun you've had since you graduated from games to business plans and household budgets.

To a good extent the size, shape, grade, and soil of the lot on which a house sits determine the location and configuration of an addition. The structure of the house also plays a part, as do local zoning ordinances and the amount of space you need. You may be able to add out, add up, or wrap an addition around the existing structure. On the other hand, the constraints of your lot, house, and local zoning may give you only one choice.

Knowledge of the basics of architectural style and design are key to whether an addition will enhance the appearance of a house or forever look tacked on. Chapter 3 introduces some basic design principles, and will help you recognize your home's architectural style. But the best way to begin thinking about enlarging a home is to start looking at houses much as if they were a series of building blocks. Strip each house you see down to its basic components and observe how the architect or designer arranged the various shapes into a pleasing configuration. Then

Above: *An 8- by 14-foot window retrofit on this California ranch house provides an area for reading and relaxing. Because an exterior wall was removed, it also adds light and airiness to the remodeled kitchen.*

The owner wanted the window retrofit to improve energy consumption. The contractor, Hoddick, Berry, and Malakoff, suggested the additional improvements after calculating the benefit of new windows versus costs and the additional benefit that could be gained by adding the sunroom.

Left: *This weekend and summer house, near a harbor formed by the mouth of a river opening out to Long Island Sound, sat in a coastal flood zone. Before adding on, the owners decided to move the house to a slightly different position on a higher foundation. The house was remodeled with one addition to provide a new entry and stairhall (center) and another to provide an enlarged living room.*

Below: *New decks were added on the front and side, and a small breakfast deck was created opposite the bedrooms on the second floor.*

apply the ideas you collect from this kind of analysis to your own home.

The simplest single-story houses (cottages, bungalows, and ranches) can be viewed as squarish or rectangular boxes. Larger story-and-a-half and two-story homes are the product of stacking these modules on top of each other, turning them on end, or joining them on one or more levels to make L-, U-, or T-shaped patterns.

Architects add interest to these basic shapes by such devices as bisecting the sides of square boxes to turn them into octagons. A close examination of the homes around you will reveal other tricks of the trade.

The illustrations on pages 8 and 9 represent the kinds of homes you see every day: single-story, story-and-a-half, and two-story versions. You'll probably find an example similar to

your own home, which you can use as a starting point for your planning.

As you look at what others have done with their homes, you'll begin to see the potential of your own home more clearly. The chapters that follow will give you pointers for planning add-ons that respect the integrity of the original structure while meeting your unique needs for expanded space.

TYPES OF ADDITIONS

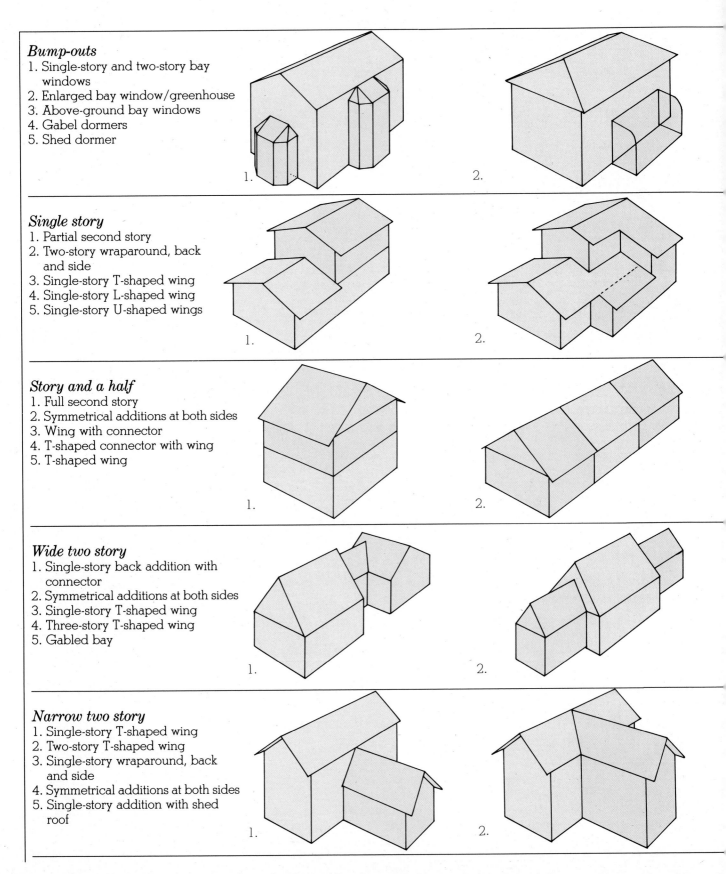

Bump-outs
1. Single-story and two-story bay windows
2. Enlarged bay window/greenhouse
3. Above-ground bay windows
4. Gabel dormers
5. Shed dormer

Single story
1. Partial second story
2. Two-story wraparound, back and side
3. Single-story T-shaped wing
4. Single-story L-shaped wing
5. Single-story U-shaped wings

Story and a half
1. Full second story
2. Symmetrical additions at both sides
3. Wing with connector
4. T-shaped connector with wing
5. T-shaped wing

Wide two story
1. Single-story back addition with connector
2. Symmetrical additions at both sides
3. Single-story T-shaped wing
4. Three-story T-shaped wing
5. Gabled bay

Narrow two story
1. Single-story T-shaped wing
2. Two-story T-shaped wing
3. Single-story wraparound, back and side
4. Symmetrical additions at both sides
5. Single-story addition with shed roof

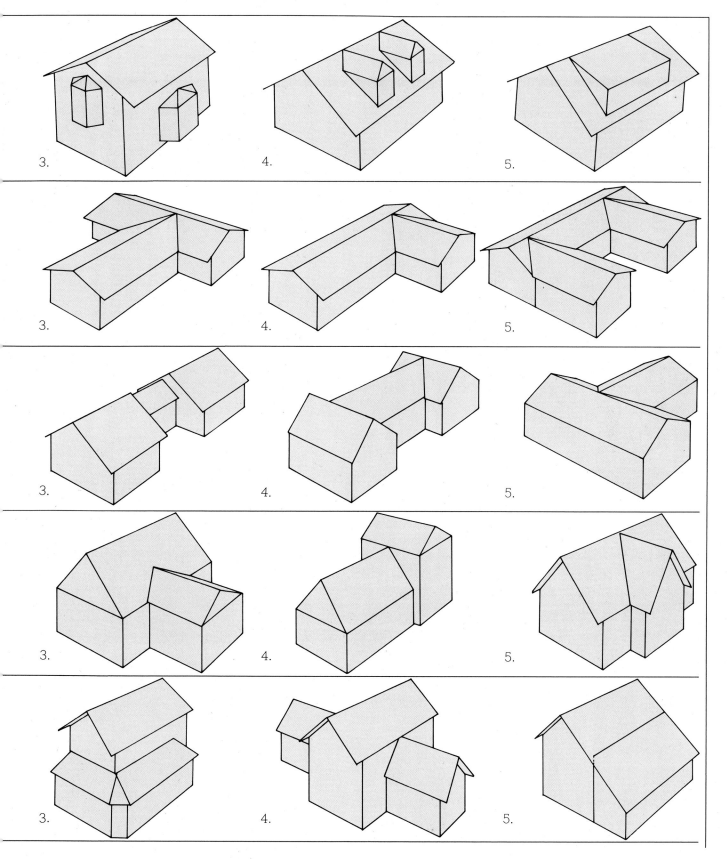

3.

4.

5.

3.

4.

5.

3.

4.

5.

3.

4.

5.

3.

4.

5.

EVALUATING A
HOME'S POTENTIAL

W*hen you begin to think about how best to meet your needs for more space, some of the most important aspects to consider are intangibles. Look at your home as a potential buyer might. Be honest in your assessment of its merits and faults. And keep in mind that even a seemingly costly addition might still be cheaper than moving to another house.*

Style. Do you like this house—its architecture and feel? It's possible to change the look of a house radically during the adding-on process, but a major change in style, although attractive, can make a house stand out disturbingly among its stylistically similar neighbors.

Neighborhood. Is the neighborhood one of the best in the area, or suffering a bit from neglect? It is not considered economically wise to overimprove your house in relation to the neighborhood. Continuity in size, material, craftsmanship, and cost along the block is desirable. A five-bedroom, three-bathroom house with a solarium and a gazebo located in a neighborhood of mostly two-bedroom one-bath tract homes would not be worth as much as if it were located in a neighborhood of similar houses. This is the single most important factor when considering if you would be able to recover the cost of your planned addition upon resale.

Schools. Even if your children are grown, the quality of the local schools will affect the resale value of your home should you want to sell it someday.

Services. What kinds of services are available nearby? Where is the nearest shopping center? Is the house convenient to public transportation and to freeway access?

The owners of this historic house wanted to replace a too-narrow back porch with an attractive space large enough for family gatherings. For their solution, see pages 42–43.

ASSESSING A HOUSE AND ITS LOT

Before you spend too much time dreaming about that new addition, you'll need to take an unbiased look at your home's potential for enlargement. You'll want to assess both the configuration of the lot it sits on and its structural soundness, as well as intangibles such as your attachment to the house and to the neighborhood.

Assessing a home you already own is similar to evaluating a house you're considering purchasing, but your familiarity with the house is a definite help. You're probably well aware of its condition, its pluses and minuses. Even so, taking the time to conduct a thorough evaluation can pay off. You may discover structural or other problems that have slipped by periodic maintenance checks, and the written notes you make during the inspection will help you pinpoint areas where assessment by a professional—a building inspector, structural engineer, architect, or contractor—might be warranted before you begin planning your addition.

If you're shopping for a new home, this kind of evaluation can help you to eliminate those houses that are not suitable for adding on. Once you've narrowed your choices down to one or two, you can call in a contractor, a designer, or an architect to verify the information you've gathered.

If you're evaluating a house you already own with an eye to adding on, it's important to determine what structural and code limitations you may have. If you're asking yourself questions like, "I wonder if the foundation would take the weight of a second story," or "Is that slope too steep to add on to the back of the house," you'll probably want to call in a professional. Still, before you make that phone call, it's wise to know the condition of your house, and to have a good idea of what you want to add and where.

In thinking about your addition, keep in mind that adding to a house can put extra stress on its structure and systems. It makes little sense to attach an addition to a house with structural flaws. To evaluate the effects of adding on, you need to know the exact condition, capacity, and expected life of your home's structural and mechanical components.

If you're shopping for a house with add-on potential, do some homework first. Contact the local building department for information about setbacks and other zoning restrictions that might limit the kind of changes you could make. Once you've narrowed your choices to two or three potential candidates, subject each to a rigorous inspection.

Allow two to three hours for a thorough home evaluation. If you're inspecting your own home, you may want to couple this evaluation with a base plan drawing of the house and lot, as described on pages 20 and 21.

Tools you'll need

Before you begin your inspection, arm yourself with the following house-assessment aids.
☐ Binoculars for looking at the roof or
☐ A ladder and rope if you'd prefer to climb up to check the roof
☐ A flashlight for checking in basement and attic corners
☐ A probe, such as a screwdriver, awl, penknife, or ice pick, for checking the condition of wood
☐ Kneepads, to make crawling under the house easier
☐ A marble, small ball, or level to check floors for level
☐ A clipboard or a notebook and pencils
☐ A metal measuring tape and graph paper, if you want to diagram your house during this inspection

Zoning, codes, and permits

Before you get too deeply into planning your addition, you'll need to gather information about the various kinds of legal limitations that could have an impact on your plans—zoning, codes, and permits. (Of course, if your plans are being drawn up by an architect or designer, he or she will be responsible for taking this information into account. Or you might hire a building consultant to do a feasibility study of what is possible, taking into account not only legal considerations but the site and structure of your house as well.)

To learn about the legal restrictions enforced in your area, call or visit your local building department. The purpose of your visit is fact-finding. You want to learn all you can about how zoning regulations and building codes will affect your plans. These laws can vary from county to county. Don't assume anything until you've checked it out.

Zoning regulations and ordinances

Zoning regulations usually affect exterior construction only, such as additions, not interior remodeling of existing living space. Zoning is intended to protect the quality of a neighborhood. In some areas, particularly those with buildings of historical interest, only certain architectural styles are allowed. Ordinances can also prevent the unsuitable use of property within a specific zone. If your neighborhood is zoned for single-family houses, for example, you're protected from any business that wants to build a factory or a fast-food restaurant right next door to you.

Zoning regulations also define the required setbacks for buildings. (A setback is the specified distance a building must be from a property line.) These distances can vary from front to back and side to side. For example, the setback from the street property line may be 25 to 30 feet;

on the side or adjoining property line the setback may be only 5 to 10 feet. You should know your property lines exactly. A fence is not an assurance of the legal property line.

Zoning laws vary widely even within the same city, and there may be other special zoning requirements in your area. For example, your zone may have a limitation that restricts how high your buildings can be. This is especially important on a steeply sloping city site.

Zoning regulations can block your plans in a number of ways. For example, if you plan a second-story addition, the restrictions may require the addition to be set back farther from the street than the first floor is. Depending on the size of your lot, this may mean that the only place you are allowed to add on is to the rear of the house. Or the zoning code may require off-street enclosed parking for your car. If so, that affects any plans to convert your garage to living space.

If you find that your plans conflict with the zoning regulations, you can apply for a *variance*, or exception to the law. Variances are intended to provide a bit of flexibility to the safety and quality standards of urban development. The permit appeals department can tell you how to apply for a variance hearing if it's necessary. Once you (or your architect) present your case, the decision is up to the local planning board.

In addition to zoning regulations, your property may have other restrictions you should know about. For example, an *easement* gives someone else, such as the utility company or local municipality, the legal right to cross your property. A *deed restriction* may be written into your deed and limit the use of your property in some way. If you own a condominium or belong to a homeowners' association, a set of conditions, and restrictions may determine what you can do

to your property. Be sure to anticipate any of these potential problems by examining your deed and checking with the building department.

Building codes

Local governments also decide what building codes apply in your area. The purpose of the codes is to ensure that you and others follow minimum standards for construction. Different codes may be in effect in different regions. These include the Uniform Building Code, the National Electric Code, and the Uniform Plumbing Code, plus any state and local codes.

The building department can tell you how to obtain a copy of the appropriate code. If you're planning to do much of the work yourself, buy a copy and study it. Usually you won't need the complete code; a condensed version or guidebook can summarize the important facts you'll need to know. Or the building department may have a publication that lists the major code provisions affecting home additions.

Some cities have new energy codes that require an entire house to conform to code if new rooms are added. In such a case, you might be required to install new windows throughout the house even if you are only adding a kitchen or a bedroom; or you might have to upgrade your heating system. Your city building code office can give you information on any such requirements.

Building permits

Most additions require one or more permits before work can begin. Permits are generally needed for any alteration that changes the structure, size, safety, or use of living space. They are usually not required for projects considered to be normal maintenance such as painting, wallpapering, reroofing (unless you remove the sheathing), or window and door replacement.

But don't attempt to interpret the regulations yourself. One of the reasons for your preliminary visit to the building department is to find out the type of permits necessary for your project. Ask if inspections are necessary and, if so, at what stage of construction. Once the work begins, an inspector will visit the site to be sure that you're in compliance with the code.

Generally the code applies only to new work that's to be done. Inspections are not retroactive. If your house is old, you will probably not be expected to bring the entire structure up to code when you add on—unless, of course, the building inspector finds something that is a definite safety hazard. Then you'll be expected to correct the situation within a reasonable amount of time. Also, improvement over a certain percentage of property value requires upgrading the whole structure to code.

You also want to find out what you need to apply for each permit. How many sets of working drawings? Can you draw the plans yourself or must they be done by a professional? If you're planning an addition that changes the exterior dimensions of your house, do you need a plot plan that shows the addition in relation to the property lines? If you're planning a second-story addition, do you need a structural evaluation from an engineer to be sure the foundation is adequate to carry the load? At what stage of construction will inspection schedules be necessary? What is the permit fee? How much time is necessary from the date of application to approval? Don't assume you can get a permit on the spot as soon as you present your plans.

Remember, this is only a preliminary visit. You're seeking information that may affect your plans. It's too early to apply for a permit. That comes later, once the working plans are finished.

The lay of the land

Start your inspection from the street in front of the house. Look at the placement of the house on its lot. Where might an addition go? Estimate the percentage of the lot occupied by the house and any other buildings. Zoning requirements often specify that no more than a certain percentage of the lot may be covered by structures.

Note the way the house is oriented on the lot. Adding to the south-facing side can increase the solar efficiency of a house, while opening up windows on a north exposure can decrease heating efficiency. Note the position of large trees, mature shrubbery, driveways, and any additional structures that could limit add-on potential. Also record the positions of neighboring homes and their effect on light reaching the house. Consider adjacent sources of noise: Is the street heavily traveled? Where are the neighbors' outdoor entertainment areas (decks, patios, hot tubs)?

Now examine the lot itself. A level lot generally offers the most cost-effective setting for an add-on. Retaining walls may be required to support structures on sloping lots. If the house is perched on a hillside, count on an expensive stepped foundation for an addition of any size.

The exterior

Begin your inspection by surveying the house from a distance. Does it sit squarely on its foundation? Look for uneven settlement, particularly at the corners. If the house has a pitched roof, does the ridge sag? Does the porch list? Do any of the walls bulge or bow? Look at the window and door frames. Are the lintels and sills horizontal and the corners of the frames square, and do windows and doors fill their frames? Look for discolorations on exterior siding, which may indicate water damage. Jot down notes about potential problems for closer inspection.

Roof. First, note the style and covering of the roof. It's generally advisable to match the roof of an addition to the style and material of the original. Next, check the condition of the roof. You'll probably be looking at asphalt (also called composition) shingles, the most common roofing material in this country. Are the shingles broken, cracked, or curled? Are any missing? Is discoloration or other deterioration visible? Dark patches on asphalt shingles indicate that the surface material has worn away. Again, look for any sagging at the ridge or on the roof faces. Try to find out the age of the roof so that you can estimate its remaining life. (Asphalt shingles, for example, can be expected to last 15 to 25 years.)

Look at the metal skirting (flashing) around the chimney and vent pipes. Do they form a complete seal? Are there any indications of leaking here or where the roof faces join? Move closer to the house and look up at the eaves for obvious signs of rot or decay. Do the gutters sag? Note the position of any questionable roof areas for closer inspection from inside the attic.

Also check the condition of the chimney. Is it plumb, or does it lean away from the house? The joint between the chimney and the house should be tightly sealed. Check the mortar of masonry chimneys, and look for discolored bricks that might indicate leaks. The top of the chimney should extend 3 feet above a flat roof and 2 feet above the nearest high point on a pitched roof.

Foundation. Now walk around the perimeter of the house. Inspect the foundation, paying particular attention to any areas that appeared from a distance to be settling. Check for cracks—particularly vertical ones larger than $1/4$ inch—in poured concrete or masonry foundations, and examine the mortar between bricks. The foundation should be exposed for 6 to 8 inches above ground.

Peeling paint on a concrete foundation may indicate moisture build-up in the basement. Soil should be graded away from the foundation to channel runoff water away from the house. Look for signs of runoff pooling against the foundation. Check to see that downspouts have splash plates to channel water away.

Inspecting the roof: safety first

Although it's possible to get a lot of information about the condition of a roof by inspecting it from the ground with binoculars, you may want to climb up on a ladder for a closer look. If you do, be sure to observe these safety tips.

☐ On the ladder and on the roof, wear soft-soled shoes, such as tennis shoes, to minimize the chances of slipping. Soft-soled shoes will also do less damage to the roof than will heavy work boots.

☐ Wear a loose, comfortable shirt and pants so you can move around easily.

☐ Before using a ladder, check that all the rungs are solid and that there are no loose screws or rivets. Set the ladder up according to the manufacturer's instructions, making sure that the feet are level and firmly set.

☐ If you're working with an extension ladder, keep it from slipping to the side by tying the top to a gutter support strap.

☐ Don't lean out when you're standing on a ladder; keep your body inside the ladder rails.

☐ If you're inspecting a steep roof from top to bottom, tie yourself to a rope that goes over the ridge and is secured on the other side to a tree, porch upright, or the like.

☐ Don't go up on the roof when it's raining, when the roof is wet, or if a lightning storm is imminent.

☐ Finally, if you're nervous about being on the roof or high on a ladder, don't force yourself to do it.

The anatomy of a house

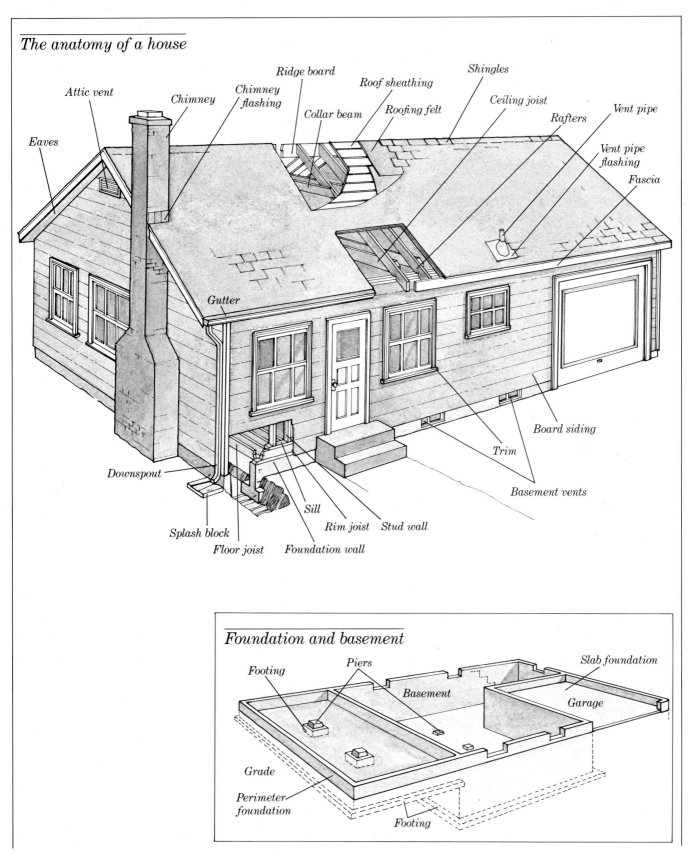

Attic vent

Eaves

Chimney

Chimney flashing

Ridge board

Collar beam

Roof sheathing

Roofing felt

Shingles

Ceiling joist

Rafters

Vent pipe

Vent pipe flashing

Fascia

Gutter

Vent pipe

Board siding

Trim

Basement vents

Downspout

Splash block

Floor joist

Sill

Rim joist

Stud wall

Foundation wall

Foundation and basement

Footing

Piers

Basement

Slab foundation

Garage

Grade

Perimeter foundation

Footing

Look for the fuzzy white columns of termite tubes snaking up the foundation. Termites and dry rot can destroy wood from inside, with little visible evidence. Examine any wood adjacent to the foundation, such as siding or porch supports. If you question its soundness, probe it with your screwdriver. If the wood feels like cork, it's seriously rotted.

Foundation depth is determined by local temperatures, soils, and the height of the house. If you're considering adding a story, the original foundation may require beefing up, an expensive proposition.

Siding. Note the type (wood, stucco, aluminum, vinyl, masonry) and the condition of the siding. If the siding is in poor condition, re-siding the whole house will increase your options for changing its look—but it will also add to the expense of the addition.

Carefully check wood siding for rot (especially the bottom courses along the foundation), and for bubbled or flaking paint, which may indicate insufficient ventilation of the home's interior. Note bulges or cracks in stucco; deteriorating mortar between bricks or stones as well as breakdown of the bricks; and dents, chips, or cracks in aluminum or vinyl siding.

Gutters and downspouts. Look up to spot holes in gutters. Watch for sagging. Note any discoloration of siding where gutters and downspouts meet, and any missing or broken downspouts. Check these areas closely during your interior inspection. If you are up on a ladder to inspect the roof, check the gutters for evidence of overflow. Do they have screens or baskets to catch leaves and other debris?

Windows and doors. Note the type of windows and doors; you'll probably want matching ones for the addition. (For an illustrated comparison of various types of windows and doors, see pages 26–27.)

Check the caulking between window and door frames and the siding, probe wood frames for rot, and check that windows and doors are snug but not sticking in their frames.

The interior

Start your inside examination at the bottom and work your way up.

Basement. An unfinished basement provides the best clues to the overall condition of a house because foundation and framing are exposed, but even a finished basement can tell you a lot.

Does the basement smell musty or feel damp? Look for signs of moisture—discoloration along the lower wall surfaces; a powdery white or multicolored efflorescence on exposed concrete; damp wood sills or discoloration of framing members. Check the location of any foundation cracks you identified on your external examination. Does water appear to have entered through them? If you are looking for a house to buy, ask questions of the owners if you see tools or stored furniture raised off the floor.

Probe all questionable wood for rot or insect infestation. Carefully inspect the wood sills (these rest on the foundation and support the wall framing). Any water leaking down through the outside walls will end up here. Check the floor joists where they rest on foundation walls or the sill, framing supported in concrete pockets, and wood posts resting on a concrete floor or concrete piers.

Now look up at the basement ceiling. Dark stains on floor joists may indicate dry rot. Do the floor joists sag? Are water marks visible on the subfloor above the joists? These might indicate leaks in the kitchen or first-floor bath.

The basement is the best place to identify structural (bearing) walls in the house above. Most homes have at least one interior bearing wall in addition to the exterior bearing walls. It generally runs the length of the house and perpendicular to the floor

Problem house

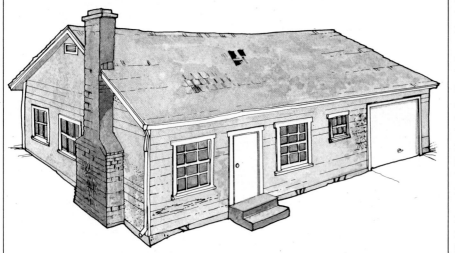

Uneven settlement of foundation, especially at corners.
Cracks in foundation.
Sagging roof ridge.
Sagging or listing porch.
Bulging or bowing walls.
Out-of-horizontal door and window frames.
Discolorations on siding.
Shingles loose, broken, cracked, curled, missing, discolored.

Sagging gutters.
Chimney leaning, not plumb.
Chimney brick discolored.
Mortar crumbling.
Soil graded toward instead of away from foundation.
Termite tubes.
Rotted siding.
Bubbled or flaking paint.

joists, often where they overlap. Any interior wall with a girder, post, or foundation beneath it is probably a bearing wall. Removing all or part of a bearing wall to permit an addition will mean extensive structural work to replace the support.

The basement can also be the best place to examine the condition of the existing plumbing, wiring, and heating systems.

Plumbing. If your addition might include a sink, toilet, bathtub, or water-using appliance, you'll want to check the adequacy of the plumbing. The line entering the house (the supply line) should be at least 1 inch in diameter, and it should not be lead (gray in color). Copper pipes are desirable. Most building codes allow plastic pipe for drain-waste-vent systems (the line leaving the house) in single-family homes, but there are usually some restrictions.

Check the condition of all exposed pipes for evidence of rust, corrosion, or leaks. If the pipes are galvanized iron (also gray in color), layers of sediment and corrosion inside may be restricting water flow. Also consider the size of the water heater. A family of four requires at least a 40-gallon tank.

Look for insulation on the hot water pipes. Older systems may be wrapped with asbestos, which can be a health hazard if disturbed. Asbestos insulation looks like pressed paper or cardboard, and is usually gray in color. Disposal can be costly, as most landfills and dumps will not accept this material.

Check the water pressure throughout the house by turning on an upstairs faucet and shower and then opening the kitchen tap. Does the water trickle to a halt? Also try flushing the toilet and running the shower at the same time.

Wiring. The house should be supplied with at least 100-ampere, 240-volt (three-wire) service to handle modern appliance loads. Check for three-wire service where wires from the utility pole attach to the house. You can tell by checking the service

panel near the electric meter whether the house has modern circuit breakers or fuses, and how many circuits it has. An add-on will likely require a new circuit to serve it; expansion blanks may be available on some service panels.

Also look for evidence of frayed or bare wiring in the basement, and in the attic.

Heating. Finally, consider the type and age of the heating system. It may prove inadequate to serve a large addition, and a separate heating unit may be most cost effective.

Check the distribution pipes of older gravity-type warm air furnaces for the presence of asbestos insulation. Breaks in the pipes can permit asbestos particles to travel throughout the house.

Living spaces. This is the fun part of the inspection. Start by siting down the floors. If they appear to slope, use your marble, ball, or level to check. Look for cracks at the corners of door and window frames, in exterior corners, and across ceilings. Write down the location of major cracks and check for structural causes. Open and close doors and windows; binding can indicate uneven settlement of the foundation or sagging in the structure of the house.

Acoustical ceilings in homes built before 1979 may contain asbestos. Any deterioration or disturbance will free hazardous asbestos particles into the air.

Note how much light enters each of the rooms, and consider how an add-on might affect that light. Bump-out additions and skylights can let more light into otherwise dark rooms. Without proper planning, however, adding on to the only side of the house that receives good light could darken existing rooms.

Attic. Inspect an unfinished attic for leaks, and check rafters and wall studs for water stains or rot. Use your flashlight to look through the rafters at the discoloration or water damage on wall sheathing. Check the chimney for aging mortar and cracks or breaks in its skin.

Service panels

Expansion blanks

Main fuse block

Identification sheet

Three-wire service head

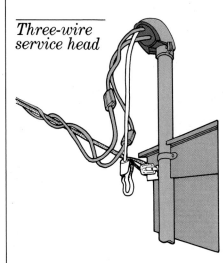

HOME EVALUATION CHECKLIST

Exterior evaluation

Orientation of house	N S E W
Evidence of settling	_____
Distance to lot boundaries	Front _____ Sides _____ Back _____
Lot	Flat? _____ Sloped (gentle/steep; direction)? _____
Landscape	Trees/plantings to preserve? _____
Retaining walls	Drainage (weep holes) adequate? _____ Leaning toward slope (good)
	rather than away from slope (bad)? _____
Other structures (location, light)	_____
Sources of noise	_____
Best/worst views	_____
Electric service	Three-wire? _____ Entrance location _____
	Ground in place (wire from service panel to brass clamp in soil)? _____
Roof	Material _____
	Age _____ Condition—sags/low spots in ridge/faces? _____
	Covering missing/worn/warped/cracked/lifting? _____
	Flashings (chimney/vent pipe/roof valley/skylight/dormer) intact? _____
	Gutters missing/sagging/cracked/rusted/peeling? _____
	Vents (at eaves/gables/ridge)? _____
Chimney	Leaning/bowed? _____
	Condition—masonry (deteriorating bricks/stone/mortar?) _____
	Chimney-house joint tight? _____ Liner and cap? _____
	Height above roof _____
Siding	Material _____ Age _____
	Condition—discoloration? _____ Missing/cracked/peeling/warped/
	dented/rusted/rotten/deteriorating (especially adjacent to foundation)?
	_____ Joints tight? _____
	Shrubs/vines against siding? _____
Foundation	Material _____
	Amount visible _____ Soil graded away from? _____
	Downspouts intact/drain to splash plates? _____
	Condition—large cracks (location)? _____
	Discolored/wet? _____ Paint peeling/blistered? _____
	Mortar crumbling? _____ Insects or insect damage (termite
	tubes/rot in adjacent wood) evident? _____
	Settling/leaning/buckling (location)? _____
Windows	Frame material (wood/metal/coated wood)? _____
	Style _____
	Condition—cracked/broken glass? _____ Frame material/finish
	intact? _____ Caulking sound? _____ Weatherstripped? _____
	Frames square? _____
Doors	Material _____
	Condition—tight/square in frames? _____ Weatherstripped?
	_____ Paint/finish intact? _____
	Thresholds rotted/swollen/uneven? _____
Trim (windows/doors/decorative)	Material (wood/metal/other)? _____
	Missing/rotted/needs caulking or painting? _____
	Special features (cornices/columns/shutters)? _____
Porches, decks, and patios	Attachment to house sound? _____ Supports (wood/concrete)
	sound? _____ Do wood supports rest on ground? _____
	Stairs and railings sound? _____
Garage	Door sound/operates smoothly? _____ Header over door opening
	sagging/bowed? _____ Slab cracked/heaving? _____
	Roof sound? _____ Spacing (inches) between wall studs _____

Interior evaluation

Basement or crawl space Foundation walls—large, open cracks visible? _____
Bowed/leaning? _____ Damp/wet/watermarked/discolored/
efflorescence? _____
Wood—in contact with soil? _____ In contact with cement? _____
Signs of rot/insect damage? _____
Ceiling—sagging/split/decaying floor joists? _____
Signs of leakage from kitchen/bath above? _____
Floor—evidence of moisture/flooding? _____
Cracks in slab (location)? _____
Concrete piers in place (directly under beams/girders)? _____
Ventilation (especially if crawl space) adequate? _____
Signs of condensation/leaking around windows or on walls? _____

Plumbing system Location of main drain _____
Location of water supply entry _____
Location of main plumbing run to existing kitchen/bath _____
Main shutoff valve working? _____ Pipes—rusted/corroded/crusted/
heavily patched/sagging? _____ Hot water pipes insulated?
_____ Capacity of water heater _____ Sufficient? _____
Waste disposal to city sewer or septic tank? _____

Heating system Type _____ Age _____ Location _____
Rated output (BTUs/hour) _____ Provides adequate, evenly distributed
heat? _____ Emits odors/fumes? _____ Heating ducts insulated? ____

Electrical system Location of service and branch panels _____
Rating of main service panel (60/100/150/200 amps) _____ Fuses or
circuit breakers? _____ Frequent overloads (blown fuses/
tripped circuit breakers) or flickering/dimming of lights? _____
Wiring frayed/corroded? _____

Living spaces Signs of settling—cracks in exterior corners? _____
At corners of window/door frames? _____ Across ceiling?
_____ Bulging or bowing walls? _____
Doors/windows open and close freely? _____
Signs of moisture/leaks—on ceiling below baths? _____ On wall-
coverings? _____ Around windows/doors? _____ Floors—sloping?
_____ Springy/spongy? _____ Creaky? _____
Staircases—framing sagging? _____ Out of square? _____
Decaying/damaged stairs/rails? _____ Creaking treads _____
Fireplace—masonry cracked/loose/deteriorating? ____ Mortar missing/
crumbling? _____ Flue lined? _____ Coated with soot? _____

Bathrooms and kitchen Ventilation adequate? _____
Signs of leaks/water damage—deteriorating/cracked/missing/stained wall-
coverings? _____
Buckled/decaying floor covering? _____
Water pressure adequate/weak? _____
Drainage adequate/sluggish? _____

Attic Structural—sagging/cracked/rotted rafters? _____
Decaying roof decking/wall sheathing? _____
Signs of leakage—on roof decking? _____ On rafters? _____
Around chimney/vent pipes? _____ On wall sheathing/studs?
_____ Light visible through roof? _____
Ventilation—gable/eave/roof vents absent/blocked? _____
Evidence of moisture/condensation (damp insulation)? _____
Vent pipes exhaust in attic? _____
Depth of insulation in floor _____

THE BASE PLAN

Before you begin to plan and design your addition, you need to have as much exact information about your existing house as possible. The evaluation checklist on pages 18–19 will show you what you've got; but creating an addition requires translating your three-dimensional house into two dimensions: the base plan. This plan will be a valuable aid; not only will it help you get familiar with the details of your present layout and make the relationships of the spaces clear, it will help you to visualize your addition.

If you already have a base plan or blueprint of your house (obtained from your builder, a former owner, or the city building department), you can use that instead of drawing your own. However, you will still have to make sure that it is drawn accurately, and incorporate into the plan any changes that have already been made. You'll also probably want to copy the plan onto graph paper, because the smaller scale and more manageable size will make it easier to plan your addition.

If you have no base plan, you'll need to draw up your own from scratch. Doing it yourself has the benefit of making you thoroughly familiar with every corner of your existing house, and with the possibilities for adding on to it.

Your base plan will be a scale drawing showing the floor plan of your house, including all rooms; walls, windows, and doors; stairs; closets, storage areas, and cabinets; appliances such as stove and refrigerator; plumbing fixtures such as sinks, bathtubs, showers, and toilets; water heater, air conditioner, and other electrical devices; and electrical outlets and plumbing lines. Imagine that you have taken the roof off your house and are looking straight down into it. Make a separate plan for each floor of your house.

The tools you'll need to draw up your base plan are simple: a 20- or 50-foot steel tape measure, a pad of graph paper, and a soft-lead pencil. At this stage, you will draw your plan freehand, using the graph paper to keep the proportions accurate and writing the dimensions on the plan as you go along. A convenient scale for most plans is $1/4$ inch to the foot. Be sure to note on the plan the scale you are using.

Begin drawing your plan with any room you choose. In orienting the first wall line on the paper, be sure to leave enough room to draw in the entire house. Draw the plan with north at the top or on the left side of the paper; this standard practice will help others reading your plan to orient themselves to the site.

In each room of your house, start with overall dimensions and work down to details. Begin by measuring the length and width of the room. Measure the distance of doors and windows from a corner or the end of a wall and from each other. Measure the width of their moldings or trims. Draw a line for each wall, leaving the proper amount of space for each door or window. Draw a second line outside the first. These parallel lines indicate a normal 4-inch wall. Fill in the space between the two lines with solid penciling.

Next draw in the doors. If a door swings, show it in the open position, drawing a quarter-circle from the hinges. Make a semicircle if the door swings both ways. For sliding doors,

draw in the fixed one, and then indicate whether the sliding one is inside or outside the fixed one, and show it about halfway open. For folding doors, show a series of little w's to the depth of each panel. Show pocket doors half open, sitting within the

Drawing supplies

Although you can turn out adequate rough sketches with nothing but a pencil, a straightedge, and graph paper, there are some simple tools that will make your task easier.

The *architect's rule* is such a helpful tool. It translates dimensions directly into whatever scale you want to use. For example, if you are using a scale where $1/4$ inch equals 1 foot, the architect's rule would represent a 7-foot length as $1 3/4$ inches. Other useful drafting tools are *triangles, circle templates,* and a *compass,* which will help you make uniform angles and circles.

Hold your graph paper in place on a table or desk with *drafting tape.* This differs from masking tape in that it comes off easily without tearing the paper. Be sure the graph paper is lined to the scale you intend to use. For example, if your plan uses $1/4$ inch to represent 1 foot, buy graph paper with $1/4$-inch squares. It can be very distracting if the paper is lined to a different scale than the one you are using.

You will also need *tracing paper* to use over your base plan for experimental drawings.

For early freehand sketches, a *soft lead pencil,* one marked B or F, is best. *Harder pencils,* such as H or 2H, make finer lines and are more suitable for final sketches and working drawings.

Finally, you'll need a 20- or 50-foot *metal tape* with a locking device to measure your rooms as you draw your base plan.

stud wall pockets. Draw in the windows, showing the way they swing. Use the half-open position for sliding windows.

Measure the width and depth of cabinets, closets, and other built-in storage areas, indicating the swing of their doors. Measure and draw in floor grilles. Measure the hot water heater, furnace, air conditioner, and any other electrical devices and draw them in on your plan. If there is a door leading to their space, measure and draw in the length and direction of its swing. Note the location of all outlets, light switches, and light fixtures. Indicate where water and gas lines enter the house.

Remember that the purpose of this first, rough drawing is to gather information. Details like door swings and light switches don't need to be drawn perfectly at this stage.

Once you've recorded every significant detail on your base plan, get a clean sheet of graph paper and transfer the plan, making this version more precise. Use the architect's rule to scale off dimensions; use triangles to draw angles; and use a template or compass to draw circles. Use a compass spread to the width of the door to indicate its swing.

This plan will become the basis on which you will design your addition, so you'll need several copies of it.

Should I obtain professional advice?

Consulting with a professional before you begin to plan your addition can ease your mind about the feasibility of adding on, and it may reduce the amount of research you'll need to do during the planning process. It's up to you to decide whether a professional evaluation is in order at this point.

If you are confident about the structural integrity of your home and there's clearly room on the lot to expand, a professional evaluation may not make sense now. On the other hand, if you uncovered foundation or structural problems during your inspection, or if the only direction for expansion is down a steep hillside or on top of the existing house, consulting a professional at this point will give you a clearer idea of what will be involved in adding to the house. If you're purchasing a house to enlarge, it makes sense to get a professional opinion before you buy.

Building inspection firms can verify your findings regarding structural condition. They may also be able to advise you about foundation modifications that might be required to support an additional story. If the lot is steep, or if you plan to add a substantial load to a home's foundation, consider an initial consultation with a structural engineer or a soils engineer. Architects and contractors also perform inspections. In Chapter 5 you'll find more information about what various professionals do, and about working with them in the planning and design process.

Rough base plan

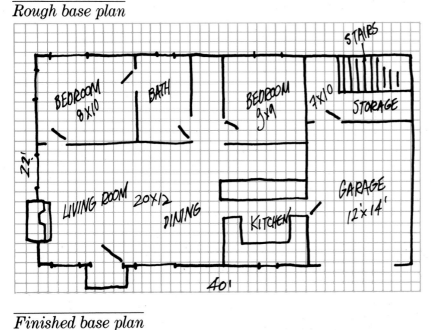

Finished base plan

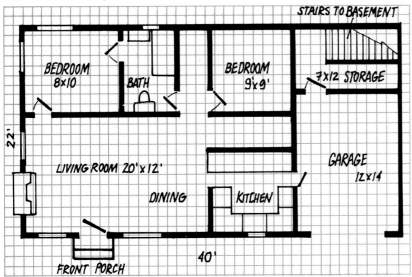

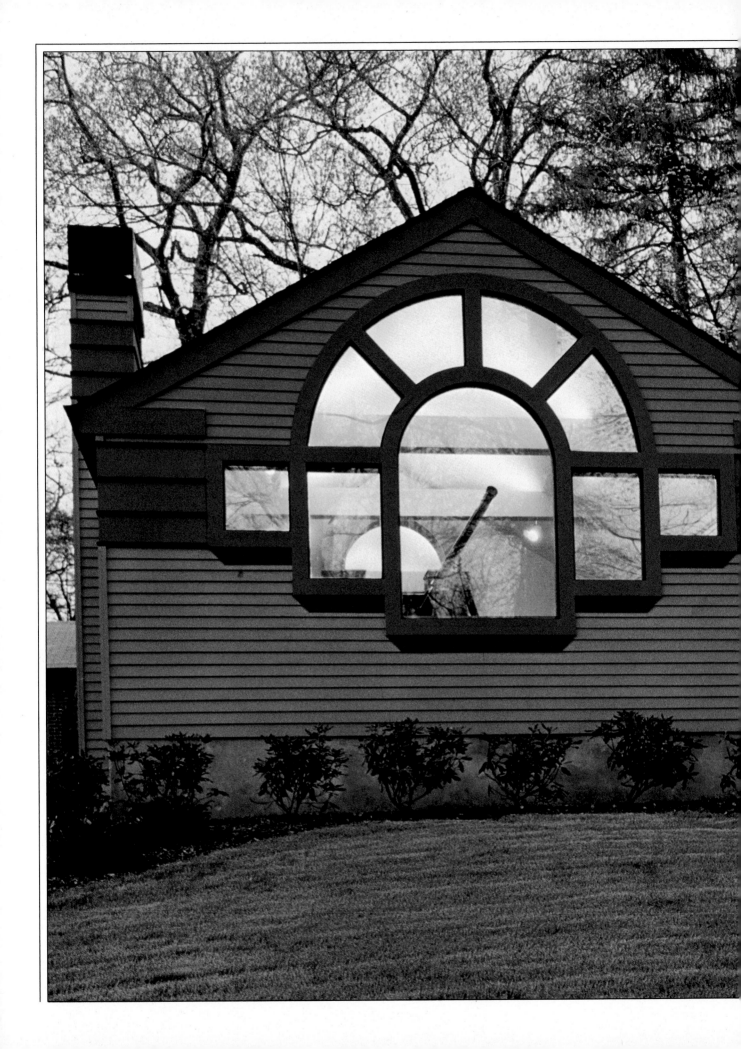

DESIGN AND STYLE BASICS

I f you were asked to identify a building that shows good design basics, you'd probably choose one that is visually satisfying and that also "feels right" in its proportions, materials, and placement. Good design, whether in a new house or an addition to an older one, is more than the end result of carefully drawn plans carried through construction to completion. Good design involves integrating certain fundamental principles of architecture into a unified form.

Thoughtful design considers balance, symmetry, and rhythm—in the building as a whole and in the arrangement of its parts. It addresses line and shape; attends to the interaction of pattern, texture, and form; and recognizes the importance of continuity of materials while allowing for deliberate contrasts. In seeking to achieve an integrated whole, good design considers more than exterior features—houses, after all, are not lived in from the outside. By defining the spaces we inhabit, design also forms a kind of framework for our lives.

This chapter will help you begin thinking about the basics of design and style as they relate to adding on. It starts with a short introduction to three fundamental principles of design. Next, it discusses common design problems that face everyone who adds to a house, and examines some solutions. Finally, to help you recognize the architectural style of your own home, the chapter concludes with an illustrated portfolio of some of the most familiar American architectural styles.

This music room addition to a Connecticut home reflects the style of the Italian architect Andrea Palladio, from whom the Palladian style window derives its name. For more details, see pages 44–45.

According to pioneer interior decorator Elsie de Wolfe, at the core of successful design lie three basic principles: proportion, simplicity, and suitability. Let's look at what each one means in the context of adding on.

First, an addition design should have proper *proportions*, from both the architectural and the visual points of view. In design, proportion refers not to exact mathematical ratios, but rather to the way the various design elements relate to each other and to the whole, and to the way everything works together as a composition. An addition to a two-story house with a gabled roof needn't have all its windows and doors lined up in absolute symmetry to appear well proportioned, but if the new wing is added at the side, it should have a gabled rather than a flat roof, and windows arranged in a similar fashion to the existing ones.

The second fundamental principle is *simplicity*. Even if the newly added front porch carries Colonial-style pillars, or the exterior walls of the bedroom addition wear the same decorative shingles and gingerbread trim as the existing house, the design itself should be simple in concept, functional in form, and straightforward in execution.

Third, a thoughtful design must be *suitable* in several respects. Clearly, it should fulfill the purpose for which it is intended—a recreation room added above the garage to give the kids a place of their own should be easy to get to; a breakfast room extension should have plenty of windows to enlarge and brighten a small, dark kitchen. But the design must also fit the context of the neighborhood. Consider how a second-story play-room with a loft above might block sunlight entering the single-level house next door, whereas a contemporary glass-walled breakfast area might be perfectly appropriate in a cluster of traditional homes.

Furthermore, a well-designed addition must be suited to the architectural style and mood of the house to which it belongs. The challenge here is that it's sometimes difficult to recognize the architectural heritage of a house, and hard to know which features should be emphasized and preserved and which can be altered successfully. (For an example of a successful alteration to a historic house, see pages 42–43.) The Illustrated Portfolio of American Architectural Styles on pages 29–33 will help you to identify your home's architectural roots, and will start you thinking about their relation to style and help you begin to visualize the overall look of your addition.

Some common design problems and solutions

The process of designing an addition brings with it some common problems—from maintaining the integrity of the style of the existing house, to achieving visual continuity at the juncture between old and new, to selecting appropriate materials for both exterior and interior. Because one mark of good design is integration, the solution to one problem may clarify the answer to another. Your solutions—like your addition—will be unique to your house and its lot, but knowing some of the tricks that design professionals employ can simplify your planning.

Positioning on the site

Whether you are building from scratch or adding on, a major design consideration of any site, on sloping or level ground, is solar access. In fact, one of the most common reasons homeowners add on is to gain more light and sun as well as space. Before you decide on the exact position and

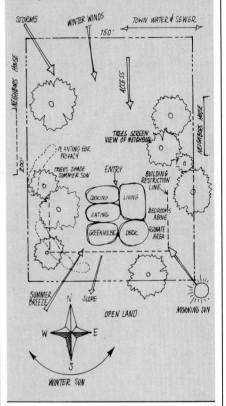

Site analysis and design

Many factors influence the placement and positioning of your addition on the lot. A bubble plan (described on page 82) will help you to define and work with those factors.

precise configuration of your addition, study the pattern of the sun's movement during the day, noticing where trees and neighboring buildings cast shadows. You may discover that placing the addition on one side of the house rather than another could make a big difference in the quality and amount of light that will enter its interior. Remember, too, that zoning requirements will influence the position of your addition—its proximity to property lines and possibly its height.

A sloping lot may or may not present a siting challenge. A gentle slope away from the house to the south is usually ideal for solar gain and encourages a design with many windows; a slope to the north, on the other hand, might call for fewer and smaller openings. You could cut into the slope and let your addition step down the hillside, following the contours of the land. Or, if you'd prefer to keep the addition on the same level as the existing house, you might extend it out over the slope, supported from beneath and accessible to the ground by stairs.

Continuity of scale
The design goal here is to retain the existing proportions of the house by neither overscaling nor underscaling the addition. Think of the addition not as a separate entity, but instead as a part of the whole. Mentally step away from the drawing board and view the house from afar. Ask yourself what scale "feels right." If the existing structure has a multigabled roof system, then the new roof may need to carry more than one peak. (For an example of a cross-gable-roof addition, see pages 60–61.) If your one-story ranch stretches out in a long, thin line, it's probably better for the overall proportions to "bend" the line by placing the addition at a right angle to the house rather than to accentuate the existing linearity.

Another dimension of continuity of scale is the "massing" of the parts of the structure in relation to each other. If you are designing a second story for a house with lots of large windows, the windows on the new upper level will need to be sized and scaled to feel at least as light in apparent weight as those on the lower floor, in order to keep the building from seeming top-heavy. If, on the other

hand, your house resembles a three-story block with a hip roof, a low, flat extension will probably look like an afterthought—a little tail on a big animal.

Symmetry and rhythm can be regarded in the same manner. If the original windows and doors are arranged asymmetrically, look for ways to place the new openings in a non-symmetrical pattern to keep the whole building in informal balance. Conversely, if absolute symmetry is the order, the addition should probably exhibit that same symmetry. Often the elements of a particular architectural style follow a certain rhythm—vertical bands of brick delineating every corner of an otherwise wood exterior, for example, or window groupings of twos and threes on each floor of a row house. In designing an addition, rhythmic patterns might be made less regular, but they should not be ignored.

Continuity of style
Whatever form your addition takes, the new structure should fit the style of the house itself and be sensitive to surrounding buildings. Matters of style are especially important when you're adding on to the front facade, where your new space will become part of the streetscape.

If your house is a pure representation of a distinct style, you can select its most distinguishing features to repeat in your design. Rooflines and window configurations—two elements that define a home's style—are usually the first things onlookers notice, and it's generally wise to echo

their shapes, sizes, and arrangement as faithfully as possible. If, on the other hand, your home is an amalgam of styles, as are many suburban dwellings built in the past 25 years, select a prominent motif—perhaps the arches of the front porch, or the decorative half-timbers on the exterior walls—and repeat that theme.

In a historic building with a well-established architectural style—a Colonial built in 1800 with Federal features, for example, or a turn-of-the-century adobe ranch—the ideal solution (especially from the preservationist point of view) is to make the addition an authentic reproduction. But finding the right materials can be a monumental task, and, more often than not, the whole reason for adding on is to modernize an old house. One answer is to create an addition that echoes the original style without trying to mimic it—a solution that may require the advice and expertise of a design professional to avoid a tacked-on look.

You can take a more relaxed approach to continuity of style in an addition that's not visible from the street, as long as the add-on is sympathetic to the overall design of the house and to its neighbors. Often an "invisible" location at the rear (for an example, see pages 64–67) offers an opportunity to treat an older style in a more modern manner: to better suit living patterns, open up a confining floor plan, or bring natural light to an otherwise dark interior. A new wing that faces front and rear can show to the street the same windows and shutters found on the rest of the facade but make use of sliding glass doors at the rear to open the interior to the backyard.

After careful thought you may decide to step away from the existing style—perhaps to add contemporary zip to a tired and outdated design, or to bring a distinctive look to a house with no clear architectural roots. In such a situation a design professional can help you establish what variations in style will work functionally and aesthetically.

Placement of elements

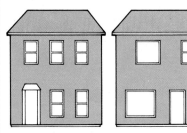

Symmetrical   Asymmetrical

Massing of elements

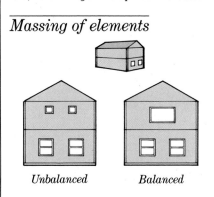

Unbalanced   Balanced

Types of roofs

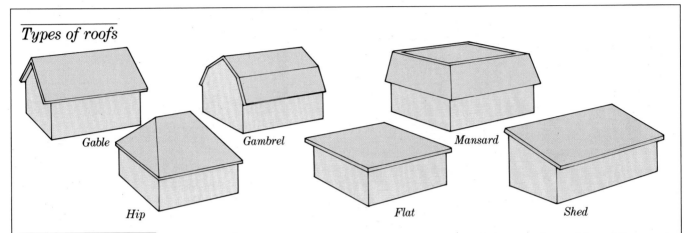

Gable

Gambrel

Mansard

Hip

Flat

Shed

Continuity of roofline

The roof system of your addition will be influenced greatly by the style and material of the existing roof and by the size and configuration of the spaces you're adding. Depending on the place where the addition joins the existing structure and the angle at which it does so, the roof connection may be continuous or intentionally different. If an existing roofline can be extended to cover the addition, the transition can be almost invisible, especially if new materials are matched to old using a staggered seam. On the other hand, a variation in height or angle between old and new roofs might be better handled by acknowledging the difference rather than attempting to cover it up—accentuating the height or angle, perhaps, or changing the direction of the roofing materials. (For an example of an addition that accentuates height, see pages 40–41.)

Placement of windows and doors

The arrangement of windows and doors has a lot to do with the appearance of a house; it's often an important clue in establishing architectural style (see pages 44–45). Generally, windows and doors in an addition should line up with those in the main building, and should carry the same proportions and scale.

But windows and doors are also the connectors between indoor spaces and the outside world, and the needs and preferences of a home's occupants sometimes conflict with architectural style considerations in determining their size and placement. There are several solutions to this kind of problem. One possibility is to match streetside windows and doors to the building style and suit the less visible openings to interior demands. If you intend to take advantage of solar gain in your addition, windows and doors must be sized and positioned to do the job, regardless of style.

Another possible solution is to vary the dimensions of windows and doors but keep style and scale unchanged. If your present house has small, multipaned, double-hung windows and you want a larger view of the world from the addition, you could substitute either a single picture window of the same size, or devise an arrangement of the same double-hung windows flanking a fixed multipane.

Juncture between old and new

The joining of existing house and addition may be designed to be structurally continuous, to appear continuous, or to be purposely different. If it would be difficult to make a smooth transition between old and new—perhaps because matching the home's exterior materials might be too expensive—consider creating a "negative space" at the junction by offsetting the addition slightly, either forward or back. This shift in position simplifies the roofline transition as

Continuity of roofline

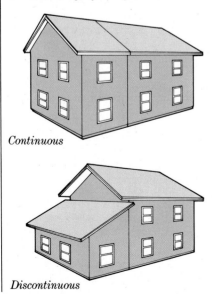

Continuous

Discontinuous

Placement of windows

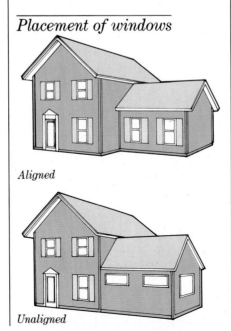

Aligned

Unaligned

Types of windows

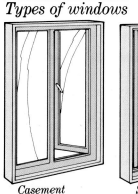
Casement

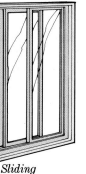
Sliding

Double hung

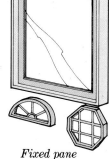
Fixed pane

Awning

Louver

well. From a purely visual point of view, the little "jog" also helps the old materials merge into the new. Another solution is to admit to the change but treat it with restraint, perhaps marking the juncture with a tall slit window, a row of glass block, or a decorative element that suits the style of the house.

Additions that are separate entities but still functionally part of the house—a garage with a playroom above, or a master bedroom wing, for example—require a connection that's more a bridge between old and new than a juncture. (For an example, see pages 70–73.) This connector might take shape as a hall or gallery, a glass-enclosed bridge or breezeway, a greenhouse, or even a multipurpose "room between."

Continuity of exterior materials
Generally speaking, for continuity of scale, style, and appearance, it's preferable to stay with the same exterior materials as are found on your existing house. Even so, you'll still have to pay attention to pattern, texture, and color when you make your choices. Refined narrow clapboard doesn't mix well with rough-sawn boards; unblemished new brick looks out of context next to weathered old brick. When a house carries a mixture of materials—for example, stucco walls with wood trim and wrought-iron accents—use them in about the same proportions on the addition and keep textures the same. A side benefit of a mixture of materials is that it offers some flexibility in solving the problem of juncture.

If the exterior siding on your house runs vertically, it will be relatively easy to join old materials to new: you can butt vertical boards together or stagger shingles down a line. Materials horizontally applied are a little more difficult to match. Sometimes you can move from old to new by creating a subtle pattern with the same materials. Often, though, this situation calls for an intentional jog in the wall; or a decorative device may be employed to avoid resurfacing the entire facade.

Attention to materials should also include continuity of detail and ornamentation, particularly if the existing house is of an older style and carries a cornice, for example, or brackets under the eaves, or gingerbread trim. It may take a little ingenuity, some custom carpentry, and the assistance of a mail-order catalog to match new detailing to old, but the benefits to the look of your addition will make it worth the trouble in the long run.

Style and scale in the interior design
The problems and solutions outlined above for exterior design apply in large part to the interior of your addition as well. Maintaining continuity of style, scale, and materials is in one

Junction of old and new

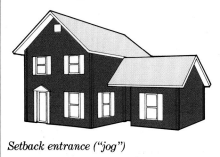
Setback entrance ("jog")

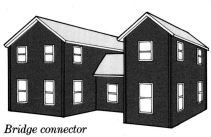
Bridge connector to new wing

Continuity of materials

Discontinuous

Continuous

sense just as important indoors as out. But there is a key difference: It's the inside of the house where the living goes on, and adding on involves both enlarging *and* improving the framework in which people live. A family-room addition can have a more open, contemporary feeling than the existing living room as long as the materials are compatible and the proportions of the new room suit the overall house design. For example, if your home features narrow casement windows on every exterior wall, you can do a couple of things to maintain the style and still make the interior of the addition more light filled and livable: Create a bay or two and line them with narrow casements of the same style; or keep exactly the same window configuration but insert skylights that are about the same size and shape as the casements into the roof.

Interior transitions from old to new

On the interior, the transition from the existing space to the addition may be handled in a number of ways. The floor level may remain the same, with only a slight shift in materials to suggest where one part ends and the other begins. Usually, though, some signs of change are inevitable, and can be turned to advantage by making them a part of the interior design. (For an example, see the homeowners' story on pages 70–73.)

Ceilings in a new room or wing may be left open to the rafters to give the room height, even if the adjoining areas retain their 8-foot ceilings. A variation in height is pleasing to the eye and gives the new space a sense of importance. If the pitch of the new roof is fairly steep, you can avoid a too-tall feeling by dropping the ceiling around the perimeter or at the corners, creating soffits for lighting as well as intimate places to sit.

Floors may step up or down at the point of connection to help ease a transition in materials or to give the new space its own identity. In a room of average size, be cautious about stepping the floor down and also

opening up the ceiling because the room may get out of scale and the proportions won't feel right. For the most spacious appearance, keep floors the same level and use partial walls to set off the spaces.

Walls in the area of transition may be designed as screens or partitions rather than as solid forms, especially when the transition occurs in a public part of the home—between kitchen and family room, or between entry hall and living room. If you must cut through an exterior wall or an interior load-bearing wall to add on, you can treat the vertical supports that remain as part of the transition—box them in wallboard, disguise them as columns, or leave them exposed as wood posts, depending on the style of your house.

Continuity of interior materials

Basically, the same rules of consistency apply indoors as out, but continuity indoors involves compatibility of materials from room to room rather than slavish repetition. The surface quality of materials is an important consideration throughout the interior. A textured wall feels heavier than a smooth one, a sanded wood beam lighter than one of exactly the same size that's rough-hewn, contoured shapes are softer than linear ones. Heavily textured walls and rough beams might be appropriate in a big playroom, but they would overwhelm a small bath. If you decide on light-stained wood trim in one room, don't switch to dark stains elsewhere. The decision about which materials are compatible, however, is a personal one that walks the line between design and decorating. (For an example of floors stained to pick up the color of the walls, see pages 56–59.)

The flow of indoor traffic

One of the most important, and sometimes neglected, considerations of good design is the circulation of foot traffic around and through the addition. It's not enough to have some extra space at the side of your lot on which to add a children's playroom if

Flow of traffic

It's wise to figure out existing circulation patterns before planning your addition. For four specific ways of adding on to this base plan, see pages 84–85.

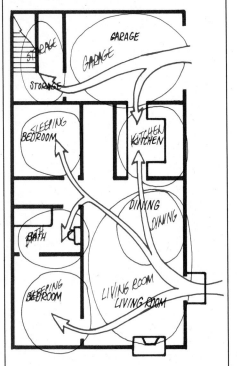

they'll have to cut through the living and dining rooms to get to it. Before you start to plan, take walking tours around your house. Try to understand the rationale behind the original floor plan. Will the addition you have in mind cut off light and ventilation, or will it improve the quality of the spaces adjacent to it? Does the location of the proposed new kitchen mean you'll have to carry the groceries from the garage through the whole length of the house? How will those who will use the space most often get to it? If the addition will be accessible to the outdoors, for example, position the doorways so that traffic won't have to cut through the center of the room.

ILLUSTRATED PORTFOLIO OF AMERICAN ARCHITECTURAL STYLES

Among the many facets of a house, its architectural styling is one of the first to capture the eye and make an impression. A particular style will show similar characteristics from house to house—for example, a distinctive roof system; window groupings; or decorative features like columns, cornices, or a special type of trim.

The style of some houses is relatively easy to identify, and you can confidently name a New England Saltbox or a Queen Anne Victorian as you walk or drive by. But most of our homes today don't fall neatly into style categories. Instead they are variations or derivations of the common styles of our American past, with motifs and characteristics blended in different patterns.

This adaptation of styles—called *vernacular architecture*—grew out of America's move across the continent, and the need of our forebears to suit their dwellings to the climates, building materials, and life-styles of new places.

Your house, and the others in your neighborhood, probably reflect this American vernacular tradition. The illustrated portfolio that follows is intended to help you identify the architectural roots from which your own house derives and to give you some guidance in deciding which features to maintain in designing your addition. With thoughtful planning and a respect for the richness of American architectural styles, your addition can contribute to the continuity of American vernacular architecture.

Saltbox

With its distinctive gabled roof that slopes sharply at the rear nearly to the ground, the Saltbox is a perfect example of a vernacular style—an architectural solution to the demands of a harsh climate and to the need for more living space. Early colonists often attached a lean-to or shed to the outer north wall of their homes; in time they incorporated that extra area into the house under a continuous roofline to serve as additional sleep or storage space and to provide a built-in buffer against wind and cold. Deriving its name from the resemblance of its long, slanted roof to the lid of the saltbox found in the colonial store, the Saltbox is sometimes picturesquely called the Catslide.

☐ The typical Saltbox is quickly recognized by a gabled roof that slopes to the rear in a long slant. In two-story designs, the roof extends to the first floor; in smaller dwellings, it goes nearly to the ground.

☐ Windows at the front, which is usually oriented to the south, are of the sash type, with 6/6 (six over six) or 8/8 multipanes; windows at the rear are small and few in number. Small dormers may project from the lower slope of the rear roof.

☐ A massive central brick chimney block is common.

☐ In New England, most Saltboxes are sheathed in shingles left to weather naturally. In some areas, the exterior often combines fieldstone end walls with clapboards or shingles.

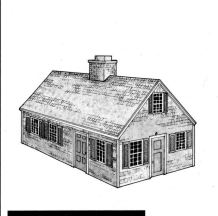

Cape Cod Cottage

The Cape Cod—as it is known in virtually every town across the country—is the typical small American house, a descendant of the little English Cottage. A vernacular style that has lost little of its charm in its travels, the Cape Cod Cottage appears in coastal towns from Florida to Maine and in the suburbs of the Midwest, complete with picket fence and rambling roses. Because it is easy to build, heat, and maintain, from the 1920s through the 1950s the Cape Cod was the most popular style in the country, later to be rivaled only by the Ranch House.

☐ The Cape Cod is a compact, 1- or 1½-story design with a gable roof of moderate pitch, sash windows with multipanes, a tidy symmetrical facade, and a simply detailed center entrance.

☐ The exterior may be of shingles left to weather to a silvery gray or of clapboards, usually painted white and dressed up with green or blue shutters.

☐ Like its New England relatives, the Cape Cod displays a massive chimney, usually at its center.

☐ The interior plan stresses function, with a tiny entrance hall feeding to two large rooms on either side and two or three rooms at the rear. In 1½-story versions, the upper floor contains two small rooms tucked beneath the gable.

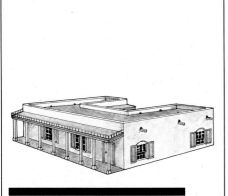

Spanish Colonial/ Southwest Vernacular

Spain introduced several strains of architecture during the early Colonial period that have left lasting impressions on our vernacular styles. The Spaniards first settled along the Florida coast, but the greater concentrations of people and buildings occurred in the Southwest in the territories that became New Mexico and California.

☐ The regional styles of the Southwest were adapted to the dry, semiarid climate and local materials.

☐ The low-profile, single-story design is arranged around a courtyard system, often in a squared U-shape, with covered porches along the inner walls to provide shady walkways.

☐ Materials are chosen to withstand climatic extremes of hot days and cold nights: thick walls of adobe brick, flat roof of dried mud or packed earth, and small, unglazed windows deeply set. In milder, seasonally rainy California a slightly different style emerged with less thick walls, roof composed of durable tile and slightly pitched for better drainage, and windows enlarged for light and ventilation.

☐ This Southwest vernacular set the precedent for the ranch houses of the 19th century, and is akin to the Ranch style of recent years.

The Mission Style

☐ The early Mission style was reminiscent of the churches and missions of Texas and the Southwest—vernacular interpretations of Spanish buildings bearing Baroque influences, distinguished by curving gables, domed bell towers, arcades, ornamental arches, and plain stucco walls set off by ornate decoration.

☐ The Mission style dominated the Spanish Colonial Revival, from about 1915 to 1940, which began in California and Florida and eventually left its mark on all of the country, but elements from Mediterranean styles appeared as well.

☐ The Revival house presents a fairly low, elongated silhouette, even in two-story designs, with low-pitched gables or flattened hip roof.

☐ Materials are consistently rough-textured: white or buff stucco on walls, red-tiled roofs, dark-stained beamed ceilings, colorful glazed and patterned floor tiles, and black wrought-iron accents.

☐ The arch motif is repeated in window and door openings, arcades, and chimney shapes, and indoors in the transitions between rooms.

☐ Balconies, trellised pergolas, and especially the patio encourage indoor-outdoor living.

Early Georgian

Over the course of the 18th century, Colonial styles were influenced in varying degrees by classical principles celebrating order, symmetry, and proportion in architecture. Even vernacular styles discarded the traditions of steep gables and purely functional window and door arrangements in favor of a new shape—the hip roof—and a respect for symmetry. The New England Colonial—the Georgian adaptation of the farmhouse—was one result. The style was also commonly seen on city streets from Boston to Philadelphia, where row houses lined up side by side.

☐ The Early Georgian is a well-proportioned compact box, usually two stories in height, with its parts formally and symmetrically arranged.

☐ Windows are of the double-hung sash type, with as few as 6 or as many as 20 panes per sash. Decorative lintels (horizontal supports above doors and windows) are common.

☐ Exterior materials are usually brick, ashlar (stone hewn into squares), or narrow clapboards, assembled to give a clean, uncluttered appearance to the facade.

☐ A centrally placed paneled door, usually set off by a carved cornice or a hoodlike projection bearing a classic motif, dignifies the front entrance.

☐ Inside, rooms are laid out symmetrically off a central hall. Paneled woodwork, plainly carved, replaced the beamed ceilings and whitewashed plaster walls of earlier styles.

Greek Revival

Sometimes thought of as our first truly national style, the Greek Revival emerged around 1820. The grandest houses of the Greek Revival copied the temple form, starting from scratch or adding a grand temple colonnade along the front of an existing building. Most homes merely alluded to the Greek form: Builders added trim to the existing gable roof to resemble a pediment, or attached pilasters or vertical boards to corners to suggest columns. The Greek Revival became the most popular Midwestern style of the 1830s and 1840s.

☐ The low-gabled Greek Revival roof carries a pedimental shape, as do the dormers. When the roof of the house is flat, a false front with a triangular peak provides the temple appearance.

☐ A distinguishing feature is a rectangular transom over the front door, usually accompanied by rectangular sidelights.

☐ Trim, whether at the roofline or framing the door, is wide, bold, and simple.

☐ A portico or porch with columns is common, although the posts or squared pillars may be used in a colonnade arrangement instead.

☐ Multipane 6/6 windows tend to be taller on the first floor than on the second.

☐ Greek Revival houses, large or small, are usually painted white to suggest marble, and frequently display shutters of dark green or black.

Gothic Revival

From the 1830s through the Civil War, the Gothic Revival style appeared around the country. Sometimes called the Pointed style, its houses were "romantic" in appearance, the larger stone mansions often resembling little medieval castles and more modest dwellings suggestive of storybook cottages. The Carpenter Gothic—the picturesque "gingerbread house" and the most familiar version of this style—was the favorite plan-book cottage of the 1850s.

☐ A key characteristic of the Gothic Revival style is the distinctive roof profile: steep gables, frequently with pinnacles at the peaks; tall chimneys; and an occasional tower or spire.

☐ Another characteristic, especially of the Carpenter Gothic, is the wealth of trim—wooden fretwork, sometimes deep and intricately patterned, along the eaves and gable edges; decorative balustrades atop porches; and tracery around windows.

☐ Windows vary: multipaned sash types, leaded casements, lancet or pointed arches. Stained and etched glass inserts are common.

☐ The Gothic style is asymmetrical in shape, with projections in the form of wall dormers, bay windows, balconies, and porches or verandas.

☐ The usual materials are brick, stone, or stucco. Carpenter Gothic houses are commonly wood, sheathed in vertical board and batten. The common roof material is slate.

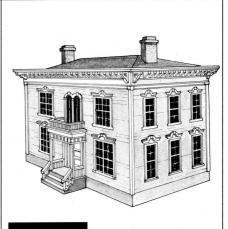

Italianate

Loosely patterned after the villas and farmhouses of northern Italy, the Italianate Style enjoyed immense popularity in the 1850s, in part because its boxy 2- or 3-story form was as well adapted to city row houses as to individual structures and could be dressed up or down according to taste. The adaptability of its shape also led to octagonal versions of the style, with the same basic size and proportions. As with the Greek and Gothic Revival styles, Italianate designs abounded in plan books of the period.

☐ The roof is hipped, with a very low pitch and wide eaves, usually supported by heavy brackets or deep moldings. An ornamental belvedere, or cupola, may top the flat-looking roof, giving it height and grandeur.

☐ The facade is formally balanced, with windows and doors symmetrically placed. A central portico or small porch embellished with detailing borrowed from Italian architecture adds importance to the entrance.

☐ Grouped in twos or threes, window openings may have rounded heads or be square at the top with rounded panes of glass.

☐ Stone and brick are the major materials, especially of the row house, although stucco is also used. Octagonal designs are nearly always wood framed and carry horizontal wood clapboards.

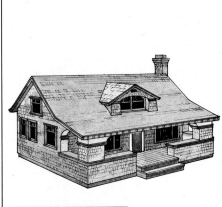

Queen Anne Victorian

In the Queen Anne, which flourished from about 1880 to 1900, elements from many past styles were woven into a rich composition. The result was a picturesque style that appeared in urban row houses, modest small-town dwellings, and mansions of lumber barons and shipping magnates from coast to coast. Larger houses in particular emphasized free-flowing interior spaces and circulation around a large informal living hall.

☐ The Queen Anne form is distinctively asymmetrical, from rooftop to ground level: steep gables, sometimes in combination with a hipped roof; second-story projections that may be gabled, hipped, or rounded; corner turrets and bays, or just rounded corners suggesting a turret shape.

☐ Horizontally arranged contrasting materials, textures, and patterns express the style's emphasis on exterior surfaces. In a typical Queen Anne, the first floor might carry stone or brick; the second, decorative boards; and the third, patterned shingles.

☐ Sheltering porches and/or wraparound verandas visually enlarge the first floor and open the house to the outdoors.

☐ Decorative details include carved wood trim and delicate fretwork painted to contrast with surface materials; fish-scale, diagonal, or diamond-pattern shingles; and stained or beveled glass inserts in transoms and upper windows.

The Shingle Style

Getting its start in New England in the 1880s, the Shingle style first appeared in small seaside resort hotels and large summer cottages. But the simplicity of the Shingle design and its emphasis on natural wood spurred the growth of the style around the country well into the 20th century. Exposure in pattern books helped foster popularity in the Midwest and far West, and laid the foundation for early Bungalow designs.

☐ Deriving both from its Victorian cousin, the Queen Anne, and from colonial antecedents, the Shingle style is broadly proportioned, with a moderately pitched gabled roof and shallow, unadorned eaves. Turrets and bays, if present at all, are integrated into the structure.

☐ Consistency of exterior surface materials—naturally weathered wood shingles, horizontally applied, usually underscored by an unobtrusive foundation of rough-textured stone—is emphasized.

☐ The horizontal line of the Shingle style is reinforced by banks or groupings of small multipane windows, distinctly Colonial in reference.

☐ Ample porches and verandas, sheltered from the sun but open to the breezes, become natural extensions of the interior floor plan and serve as outdoor rooms for living.

☐ Inside, the emphasis is on functional planning and continuity of spaces—a trend that continues in virtually every style of the 20th century.

The Bungalow

Probably the favorite small house design of the early 20th century, the Bungalow style was born in California but quickly spread across the country—thanks in part to its exposure in plan books and its availability through the Sears, Roebuck mail-order catalog as a precut kit house. The style's simplicity and adaptability encouraged regional variations. The Craftsman's Movement adopted the Bungalow form as the perfect medium to express the art of fine craftsmanship and to display natural materials at their best.

☐ Compact in shape with a gently pitched gabled roof, the Bungalow is a single- or 1½-story design, often with a prominent front porch sheltered by a low, broad gable.

☐ The front porch often carries tapered posts and/or flared base borrowed from the Shingle style. Sometimes a pergola or trellis extends outward from the roofline to ease the transition from indoors to the outside.

☐ Natural materials—cobblestone or rough-finish brick for foundation and chimneys; wood shingles left to weather naturally or lightly stained on exterior walls—give many bungalows a rustic look. Stucco-finished examples usually have a tile roof.

☐ The floor plan is as simple and functional as the style itself, with the porch leading directly into the living areas and rooms connecting to one another without wasted hallway space.

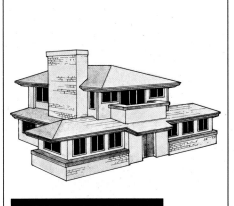

The Prairie House

So called because its rather low horizontal form was designed for the flat Midwestern landscape, the Prairie style first appeared around 1900 and represented a new concept in design—that the style of a house should reflect the needs and living patterns of its inhabitants. Its originator, innovative architect Frank Lloyd Wright, stressed continuity of space and living areas open to natural light, air, and views through and across the interior to the outdoors. By the 1920s, the Prairie style was widely built from coast to coast.

☐ A key feature of the Prairie style is a broad-hipped or gabled roof system with wide overhanging eaves that project like sunshades to help define and shelter the various living levels.

☐ A distinctive low-profile but massive chimney block anchors the structure vertically to the ground; around it, floors and levels extend horizontally like shelves.

☐ Large bands of casement-type windows introduce light and air; sometimes the windows continue around corners in a ribbon effect.

☐ Exterior walls serve as wings and protective sides for half-walled terraces and balconies.

☐ Common materials include light-colored brick with stucco ledges and coping, and stuccoed surfaces trimmed with horizontal bands of dark wood. The floor plan is open, with living areas flowing around the chimney core.

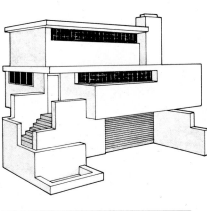

The International Style

The International style arrived in this country in the early 1930s from Europe and went on to become a significant influence on modern architecture in general and the forerunner of the clean-lined classic contemporary seen everywhere today. It is noted for its functionality, stark simplicity, flexible, modern interior arrangements, and emphasis on standard industrial materials.

☐ Easy to identify, the International style is cube shaped with a flat roof, smooth continuous wall surfaces, and an absence of cornices or projecting eaves.

☐ Most windows are arranged in horizontal ribbons or bands separated by sections of plain wall, the visual effect being that of alternating "curtains" of wall and glass. Clerestories often line the upper portion of the facade.

☐ Manmade materials—reinforced concrete, glass, steel—have precedence over natural materials; concrete sometimes carries a stuccoed or plastered finish.

☐ Although there is balance and geometry of form, the parts of the house are not symmetrically ordered—balconies and portions of the upper floor, for example, often cantilever over the ground level to varying depths.

☐ The style uses little or no ornamentation inside or out, rarely employs pattern or color, and emphasizes white as the international shade.

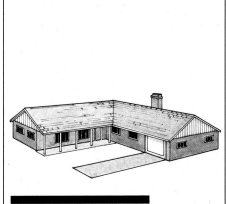

Western or California Ranch

The Ranch House as we recognize it today appeared in California around the turn of the century, a descendant of the Southwestern Ranch of the 1830s but more closely related to the gabled wood-frame houses brought West by pioneers and to the simple, functional bungalow that evolved about the same time. In the 1950s and 1960s, countless variations, including "expanded" and split-level designs, became widely available through plan books and home magazines, tempting affluent readers with larger, more elegant versions of the style. The California Ranch is an example of a modern vernacular style, and still one of the most popular houses being constructed today.

☐ Shaped as a simple rectangle, or in an L or U configuration, the Ranch is single-storied and ground-hugging, with a low-pitched gable roof that frequently projects to shelter a walkway or to create a covered patio.

☐ Picture windows and sliding glass doors bring light and a sense of the outdoors to the interior.

☐ Materials vary and may be mixed and matched. Most common are walls of stucco, wood boards or shingles, and brick; and roofs of tile, wood shingles, or composition material.

☐ The typically small floor plan usually offers an informal living and dining room, a kitchen with nearby family areas, and a patio or deck accessible from all these rooms.

A GALLERY OF AMERICAN ADDITIONS

Most American homes today don't fall into the neat style categories illustrated in the Portfolio. Instead they are variations or derivatives of the common styles of our past—styles that have changed over the years as people moved from place to place, or new building techniques and materials became available, or life-styles changed. Along the way new styles evolved that borrowed favorite motifs or characteristics from older ones and blended them together in different patterns. Your house, and the others in your neighborhood, probably reflect the influences of many styles.

In fact, most of the houses that we live in today were built since the 1930s. Many of these houses are derivatives of the styles illustrated earlier. Like the homes featured in this Gallery of Additions, your addition, thoughtfully planned and respectful of style, can contribute to the continuity and richness of American vernacular architecture.

The shingles that cover the addition will weather to the same shade as those on the original house. The slight offset in the roofline was intentional, to make a planned reroofing easier. For more information, see pages 46–47.

*Once a tiny square bungalow with a
narrow porch across the front, this San
Francisco-area house expanded to the
front and rear in three phases and
became more contemporary in style
along the way.*

A little bungalow that grew

This is the saga of a California bungalow, only 800 square feet in all, that
grew—front, back, and up—over a
ten-year period. The little house doubled in size, taking on a more contemporary style and increasing im-
measurably in comfort. The most
recent, and largest, addition rises two
stories at the rear, yet feels neither too
imposing nor too tall for the rest of
the house and perfectly at ease on its
narrow city lot.

When Kathryn Schmidt, AIA,
bought the Palo Alto, California, bungalow in 1970 (for $27,500), she had
just launched her career as an architect. She liked the 200-foot-deep private lot and the quiet side-street location just a short distance from her job
with the firm of Spencer Associates,
but she hoped eventually to tear
down the plain boxy bungalow and
build a contemporary home. Two
years later, though, she decided to
do something simpler: remodel and
expand.

The 1920s bungalow had a typical
floor plan, a functional square of
rooms with a porch across the front;
its only decorative feature was a to-
ken dormer on the gable facing the
street.

Schmidt extended the living room
by moving the wall and entry forward
to the edge of the porch, for a gain of
about 7 feet, then finished off the
other side of the porch, which had
earlier been enclosed with plywood,
to create a unified facade. At the
same time she improved and enlarged the kitchen, updating materials and appliances and incorporating
the rear service porch into the plan to
provide more storage and counter
space. The cost for that first 1972
project was $15,000.

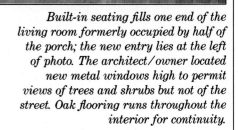

*Built-in seating fills one end of the
living room formerly occupied by half of
the porch; the new entry lies at the left
of photo. The architect/owner located
new metal windows high to permit
views of trees and shrubs but not of the
street. Oak flooring runs throughout the
interior for continuity.*

The study in the foreground is fashioned from another piece of the original porch; the step-down office beyond was added in phase two. The low skylight and large window work in concert to maximize southeastern light.

The kitchen at the rear of the bungalow also grew in stages. In the first expansion it blossomed from a narrow galley into a roomy L-shape, taking over the service porch and getting a complete facelift in the process. The breakfast bar and sitting alcove came about during the last-phase addition.

Five years later, Kathryn Schmidt was ready for a little more room and decided to add a small 10- by 12-foot study at the front. "It was about as straightforward a design as you could imagine," she says. "I simply continued the slope of the gabled roof downward, compensating for the lower ceiling inside by stepping the floor down two feet." The local setback ordinance restricted extending the room more than 10 feet into the front yard. "Luckily," says Schmidt, "that distance was perfect for the angle of the roof."

To bring light to the new room, she inserted a fixed skylight near the outer edge of the roof, lining it up with a window of similar proportions that now looks out on a small screened garden. Working with the same contractor who had completed the earlier job, she specified a simple slab foundation. The whole project took six weeks and totaled $10,000.

The last and most dramatic growth spurt for the little bungalow came in 1983. This time Schmidt decided to add on to the rear. Her objectives were to gain a second bedroom and bath, and to achieve better circulation in and around the kitchen ("a dead-end space where everyone got stuck in the corner," she remembers) by opening the room up to an adjoining eating/sitting area that would connect to the rest of the house and be accessible to the outdoors.

The addition is as wide and nearly as deep as the original 32-foot-square bungalow, vertical in form so as not to encroach on the generous backyard or interfere with existing trees, and moderately contemporary in style. Although the addition is slightly taller than the existing house, its gabled roof echoes the slope of the old. Where the two structures join, the architect employed a 16-foot-long skylight to ease the transition. Inside, that same skylight brings plentiful natural light to the expanded kitchen.

In keeping with the scale of the old house, all of the added spaces have about the same proportions—no room very large or very tall, but with slots of high spaces for visual interest. One aspect of the design theme was to provide views into the distance through adjoining spaces, and to "frame" those views with small windows. Explains the architect, "So often in a suburban setting a big picture window gives you less of a view than a smaller one because you get the neighbor's driveway along with your own yard."

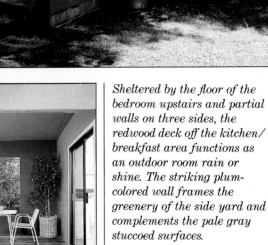

Sheltered by the floor of the bedroom upstairs and partial walls on three sides, the redwood deck off the kitchen/ breakfast area functions as an outdoor room rain or shine. The striking plum-colored wall frames the greenery of the side yard and complements the pale gray stuccoed surfaces.

A large bathroom with lots of storage was a high priority in planning the rear addition. Like the rest of the upstairs, the atmosphere is neutral, light, and airy. The green sink provides a dash of color.

A deeply recessed niche steps its way up the stairs just off the kitchen and displays the handiwork of local artisans. "It's just for fun," says the owner, "to make the climb up the stairs a memorable experience."

Intended as a tree house, the small master bedroom looks into the upper branches of neighboring pepper and walnut trees. Also visually bringing the outdoors in are sliding doors to a west-facing balcony, and a skylight-window combination that feels and functions as a single window.

The new floor plan extends the kitchen to include a counter/breakfast bar, a sitting area with an alcove, and a redwood deck that's covered by a portion of the second story. Upstairs, the plan is devoted to a bedroom—only 12 by 13½ feet, but made to feel larger by the presence of an adjoining balcony deck—and a tightly arranged bath that boasts a wall of storage and closets.

Although visually and functionally integrated into the existing house, the addition was designed to be framed and enclosed as a separate structure, in order to permit construction to proceed without disrupting the owner's life completely; interior walls were knocked out and reconfigured only toward the end of the three-month project. Costs for this final addition phase came to $60,000.

Will there be any more add-ons? "Well," admits Kathryn Schmidt, "I'm considering opening the living room upward to bring in some more light . . . ."

Customizing a tract home

When their tract-built 1960s ranch-style home partially burned in 1983, the owners made the most of their disaster-induced opportunity. Unwilling to move from the neighborhood they had known for years, they decided to dramatically change the "public" parts of the house, while restoring other spaces just as they had been before the fire.

The family had never been satisfied with the very ordinary, horizontal lines of their typical ranch house, or with the front entrance. The front door had no walk from the street, leaving only the driveway as a path from street to house. Everyone came in by the back door; the formal entrance was seldom used.

The architect, Glenn Arbonies of Centerbrook Architects in Essex, Connecticut, decided to break up the lateral lines of the existing house by adding vertical elements—dormers, bay windows, and a tall, glass-enclosed entrance vestibule. The three smaller dormers give a spacious brightness to the kitchen. The fourth, rising above the roof ridge and extending to the back of the house, makes a grand and welcoming entrance.

By moving the new entrance to where everyone entered anyway, space was created for a much-needed office for the consulting business of one of the owners. A custom-made front door of Japanese-inspired design further enhanced the entryway. The grain of the wood echoes the lines of the dormers.

Above: Rebuilt after a fire, this ranch-style house has been upgraded with four tall dormers.

Right: The spacious, well-lighted entry hall leads past the kitchen, on the right, to the dining room. This dormer continues across the house to the rear, its windows helping to bring the outdoors into the dining room.

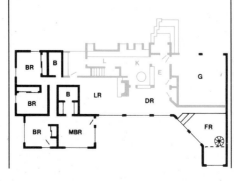

Left: *The Japanese-inspired design of the inlaid-wood front doors reflects the angles of the dormers.*

Below: *The more open revised floor plan gives the dining room a new feeling of spaciousness and comfort.*

In talking with his clients, Arbonies discovered that the heart of the household was the kitchen table. Since the kitchen had been mostly consumed in the fire, along with some of the family room, most of the dining area, and all of the garage, the architect was able to design a new kitchen. Immediately adjacent to the dining room and new entrance, the kitchen is now enclosed in glass walls, creating a transparent connection into the entire house. From the kitchen table the family can now see through the dining room into the back yard, and into other areas of the house.

New light, new space, new look—these three disaster-induced changes, blending the old with the new, make this dressed-up ranch-style house more homey and livable than ever.

A Victorian octagon that is both contemporary and authentic

The cupola-crowned octagonal wing of this Victorian-era brick house, situated on a hilltop in northern New Jersey, may look appropriately aged from the outside, but it was added just four years ago to serve as a large, informal family gathering room off the existing kitchen. The octagonal room measures 24 feet across and replaces a glassed-in porch so long and narrow that it was almost useless as living space.

The owners, a surgeon and his wife, wanted a multifunctional room, with plenty of space for visiting grandchildren to play in without being underfoot, with easy access to the terrace and backyard.

Initially the owners planned just to work with a contractor, but after some thought they decided it would be a mistake to add on to their historical home without expert advice. Designed in 1872 by Josiah Cleveland Cody, who also designed the original Metropolitan Opera House in New York City, the house is a blend of several 19th-century styles. It is influenced mostly by the Gothic Revival style, as seen in its steep roof gables, tall chimneys, and picturesque asymmetry. As the owners explain, ''We realized that in a house such as this, achieving the correct scale and proportions was very important. We didn't want to ruin the design of the original architects.''

The architect the owners selected was Robert L. Harper of Centerbrook, an Essex, Connecticut, firm of architects and planners. In designing the addition, Harper paid close attention to scale and proportion, repeating existing window shapes and exterior detailing. He drew from Victorian styles in topping the new wing with a cupola—the skylight of the era—which serves as a source of daylight for the family room and adjoining kitchen. The architect was also attentive to his clients' admiration for Thomas Jefferson's home, Monticello, by borrowing the design's domed ceiling, octagonal form, and classical motifs, and putting them to modern-day use.

For example, the vertical supports around the perimeter of the room are faced with decorative pilasters that appear to hold up the domed ceiling but are really hollow spaces that hold narrow shelves, storage, and portions of the lighting and heating systems.

The original budget for the 1982 project was $75,000; final costs came to about $85,000, due in part to an increase in the quantity of custom cabinetry and to the owners' commitment to high-quality materials and fine detailing. ''It was well worth the extra expense,'' they say, ''for in this house of tiny rooms, the new family area has effectively doubled our living space.''

The flat-roof porch that stretched alongside the kitchen of this historic 1872 New Jersey home looked out of scale with the rest of the building, and at 7 feet wide was too narrow to use.

Above: *A domed ceiling adds drama and grace to the octagonal family room, open to the kitchen in one direction and used daily for informal dining and as a place to relax. Classically carved pilasters help define the perimeter of the room visually.*

Right: *Within the rooftop cupola, eight small windows open to help with summer cooling and provide balanced light to the interior any time of the year.*

Ingenious elegance on a 16th-century note

The exacting standards of a musician and the love of a 16th-century architect's work became the challenges to fulfill in a music pavilion addition to this Connecticut home.

The owner had computed to the inch the dimensions required to deliver the proper acoustic reverberation for his grand piano, custommade harpsichord, and custom stereo sound system. The room was to be 21 feet wide, 29 feet long, and 14 feet high, with a cathedral ceiling. And the owner wanted the design to capture the spirit of Italian architect Andrea Palladio.

To achieve the desired result, architect Paul J. Pugliese, Vice President of Preiss Briesmeister Architects, Stamford, Connecticut, collaborated with the owner on design, using creative construction methods to achieve certain effects, and mirrors and special lighting to achieve others.

The new room is attached to the original house with a hallway connector that is a colonnade with a patterned tile floor and a coffered mirrored ceiling formed of recessed panels. The columns are actually painted PVC pipe. The beams that form the mirror coffers are edgelighted, giving them the appearance of floating in space. These features give the hallway an illusion of being almost double its actual height.

The design features of the music room are highlighted by the massive Palladian window and the 5- by 7-foot fireplace mantle.

The dramatic arched Palladian window is set off by wide trim, with darker paint on the lower edges to give it a three-dimensional look. The same wide trim also provides horizontal balance on the chimney.

Room lighting is concealed on top of the ceiling beams, and accent track lighting is used to highlight the English antique furnishings and the owner's collection of Chinese porcelain, Japanese woodblock prints, and contemporary art.

The owners decided on the addition after considering building a new home. Their love of the neighborhood and a comparison of values were the deciding factors. With the addition they retained a home they loved and achieved the music facility they wanted, as well as gained an improved view of the adjoining park.

Building permit variances were required for the septic tank field. Rocky ground prevented placement of the septic tank within code requirements, so the variances were granted with little difficulty.

The architect, Paul Pugliese, managed the project through construction. Problems developed with the contracting firm and a subcontractor had to be hired to finish the job, but the project was completed within the $90,000 budget. Design costs made up about 15 percent of the project total.

The colonnaded interface between old and new transcends function to make a design statement of its own. Looking toward the passageway from the music room, the arched entry and coffered mirrored ceiling give the illusion of height, and the banded tile floor reinforces the geometric emphasis of the columns.

Room dimensions and placement of the custom-designed harpsichord (to left of window) and grand piano were carefully planned to provide superb acoustics in this formal cathedral-ceilinged room. An eclectic collection of art, antiques, and porcelain is displayed to advantage. The focal-point window draws vistors' attention to the instruments, and frames an enticing view of the adjacent park.

Small apartment with a big view

A retirement apartment and desire for income-producing capability were the primary goals for this Berkeley, California, addition.

The owner, a college professor who plans to retire soon, wanted to retain the view of San Francisco Bay and the Golden Gate Bridge she already enjoyed, preserve the character of the original structure, and leave her backyard completely intact. She also wanted the new apartment to be all on one level.

The desire to retain the view dictated a second- or third-story addition, but the need for easy access eliminated any thought of adding a third story. The yard couldn't be disturbed, so the designer's challenge was to virtually suspend a 450-square-foot apartment in mid air.

A second-story sleeping porch at the rear of the house needed to be rebuilt, and this proved to be the only logical location for an addition. But its footings were inadequate for any additional weight, so new footings and pilings had to be installed. A single column was used to suspend the remainder of the addition above the yard.

The architect, George Dedekian of Oakland, California, also served as the contractor. Total cost of the addition was about $35,000, of which $4,000 was for design.

The owner admits she had no realistic idea of budget at the beginning. "I thought it should be done for half as much as it cost, and this led to some tugs of war, but now I realize I just didn't know how much things cost," she says.

Above: *The addition of a retirement apartment, with its own private entry, turned a too-large house into an income-producing property. Curved detailing on the roof echoes the lines of the original Craftsman house.*

Right: *The cantilevered second story is supported by a single column, leaving the back garden virtually undisturbed. A new back entry provides access to the main house from the garden.*

White walls, clean lines, and lots of glass give an open feel to the living room. Natural wood sills, an earthtone decorating scheme, plants, and woven baskets emphasize the natural look.

The addition incorporates a bedroom and bath from the original house with the new living room, kitchen, and entry deck. Interior design features high ceilings, large window spaces, and open railings to retain a feeling of spaciousness, and an almost continuous view of the bay.

In this particular section of Berkeley, zoning did not specifically prohibit two-family dwellings, but a special use permit was required.

The owner plans to move into the apartment upon her retirement and rent out the rest of the house.

Above: *Vaulted ceilings and spectacular quarter-round windows reinforce the feeling of living in the trees.*

Right: *The small but functional kitchen boasts plenty of storage. Wood cabinets unify the decorating scheme.*

A weekend cottage becomes a year-round home/office

The owner of this turn-of-the-century weekend cottage, set on a one-acre lot next to a pond in the Connecticut woods, wanted to develop its potential as a year-round combination home and office.

The downstairs, consisting of a kitchen and sitting room with fireplace, was a naturally insulated "Spanish fortress" with foot-and-a-half-thick stone walls. The upstairs, consisting of a living room, two small bedrooms, and a bath, was an average farmhouse of the period with no particular style and too few windows. The space was broken up and not comfortably usable. The owner, leaving the nine-to-five world in favor of working at home, decided to open and expand the living areas in a grand way with the assistance of architect Paul VanErden Reslink.

For work-related entertaining at home, the owner wanted to gain space and a gracious dining area with a view. The original living room was not quite large enough to include a dining area, and its windows were not well located to enhance the outlook toward the woods and pond.

To develop a well-lighted new space, the living room was extended and restyled. To create the feeling of spaciousness, unused attic space was transformed into a cathedral ceiling, and skylights were brought down to meet the new windows and turn the future dining table location into a nature observatory.

Off the inner end of the original living room, a tiny den was enlarged into a guest room with office alcove, a private bath, and a new deck. Doorways were repositioned, and an unused door alcove to the living room became a wet bar.

For the design of the deck next to the office, the main challenge was what to do with several trees growing near the addition, part of the graceful oak grove surrounding the house.

The owner wanted to enlarge her weekend house into a year-round home with space for office and entertaining. Redesigned rooflines blend the addition and the original house into a harmonious whole.

The original entry, **right**, had a squat, squarish porch, and the lines of the house were interrupted by shutters. The porch was removed, **below**, so that the living room could be extended to create a larger dining area.

Right: In the living room, an unused doorway provides space for a wet bar.

Below: Large viewing windows, and skylights in the cathedral ceiling, make the dining area bright and spacious.

One tree in the deck area turned out to be well past its prime and was removed; another, with a strong, handsome double trunk, became a focus of the deck design.

The deck was placed at the same height as the interior floor, with the double tree growing through it. This tree is also accommodated by an inset corner of the guest room/office.

Sliding doors, giving easy access to the deck, completed the arrangement. Now the living, dining, office, and deck areas make a single, spacious, L-shaped locale for living, working, and entertaining.

Basic to the expansion plan was the matter of making the house more elegant. This was achieved by means of rooflines and exterior wall treatment. Both additions carry gently gabled roofs, and the horizontal effect was reinforced by removing shutters to permit the free sweep of the long lines generated by the siding.

All that was needed to complete the project was landscaping. In contrast to the changes on the house, the landscaping maintains a rustic character and includes a new flagstone walk and winding stepped path between the two decks through the owner's existing wildflower gardens.

Both owner and architect are especially happy with the results. Says the owner, "It was worth every penny I invested." Architect Reslink believes that "This is an example of having very specific problems to deal with, and an owner with clear objectives—which often makes a solution more interesting and successful."

Above: *The owner's home office occupies a corner of the enlarged guest room.*

Right: *Rather than remove a fine old double-trunk oak, the owner and architect decided to save it by building the guest room deck around the tree.*

Built in 1906 but transplanted to this spot a few years ago, the original house shows its Georgian styling—symmetrical arrangement, handsome portico, and classic detailing. The "carriage entrance," right, balances the sunroom at the left.

A classic Georgian gets a new lease on life

This classic representative of the Early Georgian style and its two-story garage/bedroom addition both owe their existence to the efforts of two enterprising teachers. The 80-year-old house, located on the San Francisco peninsula, was destined for demolition until the pair offered to buy it for $2,000 and move it to a new site, and even agreed to add on a garage to meet city requirements for covered parking.

Smaller than it first appears, originally only 1,800 square feet in all, the house displays the proportions, symmetry, and classically detailed portico with pedimental roof typical of the Georgian style. Designated a historic building, and certainly worth saving, the house did have some drawbacks—tiny bedrooms and a single bath, for example—and the covered parking ordinance presented an opportunity to gain more living space over the garage.

Since city approval was required for every step of the project, the owners enlisted the services of Los Altos, California, architect Larry Madsen to develop a plan that would feature a large bedroom/bath suite over the garage, and downstairs would rework and expand an existing service porch to include breakfast, half-bath, laundry, pantry, and storage areas.

"It was important that the addition conform in scale to the existing house," Madsen explains, "but the traffic patterns had to fit, too, and the connections appear smooth and compatible." He specified new windows and doors of the same type and height as the old, used the same redwood construction and exterior siding, and designed a shallow gabled roof for both house and addition. (The original roof had to be pulled off before the move.) Inside he maintained the same proportions but used modern skylights and materials and, say the owners, "squeezed stor-

Below: Proportioned to fit the scale of the existing house—and the size of the corner lot—the garage addition to this surprisingly small historic California home features a large bedroom and bath.

age into every spare inch."

The plans for the 1981 project proceeded smoothly but the owners had to apply for a variance to retain the porte cochere—once the carriage parking spot but now a "nonessential" decorative element. "But it was essential to the architecture," the owners insist, "to balance the sunporch at the other side of the house."

In preparation for the move, the columns at the front and the porte cochere were taken down and loaded onto the deck. After the predawn journey, the house remained jacked up in mid-air for a month while the foundation was poured for old and new construction, then lowered into place with only a few bro-

ken window panes. It was a long, expensive process: $15,000 for the move; $2,000 to the utilities to lower the wires en route; and $5,000 for the foundation. The roof was also constructed during this month—in the middle of the rainy season.

Once construction was complete, the owners immersed themselves in finishing the addition. For authenticity in detailing, they created new moldings to match old by combining individual strips of trim into one piece. They selected only Williamsburg colors for the paint scheme, and painstakingly matched old floor boards to new. "We wanted to do a first-class job," they sum up, "worthy of the Georgian house."

Left: *The mood of Colonial America flavors the above-garage bedroom—Williamsburg colors of ivory, off-white, and blue, simple muslin curtains, and lace canopy and spread. The owners fashioned nearly all the moldings themselves from separate pieces of trim.*

Above: *The extra-large bathroom, with its angular shape, is a pleasant change of pace from the adjoining bedroom. The center mirror above the vanity hides a built-in medicine cabinet, and the planter screens the toilet from view.*

Left: *The breakfast room fills the former service porch; the area to the right was added to provide extra storage and a skylighted walkway to the rear patio.*

View addition to Connecticut beach house

A few years after they purchased this rambling Connecticut shoreline home—styled in the "beach house" tradition common to that area in the late 19th century—the owners decided to expand a small family room at the rear to incorporate a game area and snack bar for their teenagers. Part of an earlier addition, the room had served as a garage before previous owners decided to make use of the space and build a separate carport. "There wasn't much room left on the lot," the owners recall, "so we were willing to give up the back patio to allow for expansion, but the zoning board said no."

Disappointed, but eager to gain a new family area, they turned to architect Paul Pugliese to help find a solution. "The logical place for the addition was over the carport," he says. "For one thing, a room in that location would have an excellent view of the water." The family also liked the idea of the privacy and separation it would afford. Furthermore, all agreed that the low, flattop carport looked out of scale with the two-story, gable-roof house.

Using drawings and a model to help his clients visualize the final design, Pugliese enclosed and enlarged the carport into a garage, then placed a 500-square-foot family room above, connecting it to the upper hall of the house with a skylighted bridge. He repeated the roof pitch of the existing house as well as its overall proportions and echoed the shape of the sheltered front veranda with a deck-covered walkway that leads to the kitchen. Says Pugliese, "I extended the scale by anchoring the right side of the garage to the ground with a strong vertical mass, and by

using a screen wall and dropped beam to make the walkway more substantial and humanscaled. The new building becomes an extension of the old rather than an addition."

Inside the new family space, the design is that of a contemporary beach house, dominated by an arched window, 10 feet wide by 8 feet tall, that provides water views from nearly every point in the room. The ceiling vaults to meet the gabled roof above exposed beamwork, making the room seem larger and more open. Centered on the window, a wood-burning stove gives focus to the sitting area of the room. Other areas are zoned for game tables and TV watching, while a refreshment bar fills the front corner close to the small upper deck.

In planning and executing the 1978 project, the owners, the architect, and the contractor, Don Norgaard, of Mamaroneck, New York, kept costs to $50 a square foot. When it proved too expensive to custom-order the arched window, for example, the contractor built it on site. Pugliese selected materials that matched the older, existing ones but were moderately priced: aluminum siding, resistant to salt air; composition asphalt roofing; and windows with snap-on mullions rather than true divided panes. The only structural difficulty encountered was that the carport roof had to be fortified with five new footings to carry the weight of the second story; the walls and foundation needed little help.

The owners consider their family room addition a great success. "We had a fine architect who paid close attention to detail and a good contractor who earned our total trust," they summarize.

Opposite: *The two-story
addition at the right side of
this 1880s Connecticut beach
house takes the place of a low,
ill-fitting carport and encloses
a garage on the ground level
and a family/teen recreation
room upstairs.*

*White painted surfaces and vaulted
ceiling give the room a spacious feeling.
The door in the background leads to the
bridge connecting the addition to the
upstairs hall of the main house.*

Planned by the architect-designer owners to provide additional living space, an office, and a greenhouse looking out on the forested hill beyond, this San Francisco home retains its domestic look.

Adding on turns a split-level into a showplace

Many houses are so standard and similar that if you have special needs, it often seems that you have to build your own. But if the location you need is in the middle of a city, the best approach may be to buy a house specifically to add on to.

That's what this husband and wife team, a remodeling contractor and a designer, did with their split-level bungalow on a steep San Francisco hillside. The house is typical of thou-

sands of homes built in this area in the 1950s. The couple needed a house that could accommodate office space for the husband's contracting business and the wife's kitchen-designing business. So they bought a house that would let them add on.

The house is located on a main artery in a neighborhood that is easily accessible from anywhere in San Francisco. The backyard looks out on a tree-covered hillside, and the front gives a wide view of the Bay Area. But the house, set on a small triangular lot, was tiny—only 928 square feet. And adding to a split-level

The bedroom window commands a multilayered view: the upper level of a two-story greenhouse, the garden with its miniature teahouse, and out over the neighboring eucalyptus forest.

presented a challenge in relating the spaces and handling construction details.

The owners, architectural professionals, designed both the exterior and the interior of the addition and contracted it themselves. Among the special details are a clerestory window in the bedroom to provide light with privacy, a TV cabinet set into the wall so the screen faces the bed, and speakers built into the ceiling. White walls and pickled oak floors are relaxing after a day of working with designs and colors.

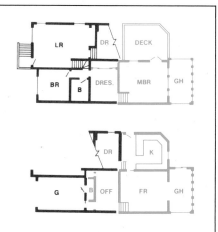

The clerestory window in the bedroom provides light while ensuring privacy. Individualized touches, such as the brass bannister, have turned this home into a showroom for the owners' clients.

Although the intent was simply for a home and office, the fact that the owners designed their own interior according to their professional standards and personal dreams turned the project into something more. With the use of vinyl windows (cleanable by tilting in), marble floors, shoji screens, brass railings, and neatly functional built-ins, their home and office also became their showroom. Clients are impressed by their design solutions and choice of materials.

The final amenities were a tiny tea garden, complete with Japanese teahouse and three cascading pools, and a two-story greenhouse of curving metal and glass, facing the borrowed landscape of the eucalyptus forest. The view from the bedroom now leads through the upper reaches of the greenhouse to the forested hillside.

Left: *The openwork fence leading from the living room to the teahouse also shelters a miniature Japanese garden.*

Opposite: *At the apex of a pie-shaped lot, the location of the teahouse solves the problem of using the available space.*

Below: *The shoji screens in the office have been lacquered to match the window frames of the greenhouse.*

The owners of this older house wanted a home office where both of them could work. The office was built on one of the last easily accessible spots for placing an addition on their lot.

A more-or-less Colonial takes one more addition

This century-and-a-half-old country house had been added onto several times, growing with the needs of previous residents. Its present owners, having just completed the sizable office shown here, are already dreaming of the next add-on, so that husband and wife can each have their own at-home work space.

Although the lot is large, the best place to build was a foregone decision. Much of the land is occupied either by wooded wetlands and a large pond, or by hillside outcroppings of bedrock, so there was really only one convenient place to build —near the problem with this location was a pair of beautiful bay windows, one of which was located where the new structure would connect to the old.

Knowing what they wanted, and where it would be placed, the owners commissioned architect Paul VanErden Reslink to help them to

visualize the addition and its relationship to the existing house. At their request, he developed a design that would allow the bay window to be salvaged and reused. Since they also

Below: The high, cross-gable-roof addition was connected to the house by means of a hallway. Rainbarrels at the four corners of the roof are functional as well as decorative.

Left: The owners wanted the office to be one large room to accommodate all of their business activities. Above the office, the high roof provides attic storage.

Below left: Inside the new office, a desk is set into the relocated bay window, providing a garden view for at-home work.

Below right: The bay window was relocated into the addition, providing stylistic continuity between the old and the new.

needed more storage space, Reslink created a 14- by 20-foot office with a high cross-gable roof, which gave the addition an attic, accessible by pull-down stairs.

The original house, with its many previous alterations, has great charm but no specific style. Vaguely Colonial, it is dressed up primarily by its windows, and by the roof trim lines and overhangs. These features, along with the white clapboard siding, were continued on the addition.

The office is connected to the house through the existing hall, and roofed at the junction with a low gable extension of the main house roof. This is followed by the high cross gable, which makes the office nicely visible from the road and drive. The resulting rhythm of lines and angles gives the house an air of distinction, and the relocated bay window now presents a view of the couple's hillside rock garden.

Financing the addition was no problem, as the bank agreed that the huge lot could well accept more house. Now with a new baby as well as new business interests, and in need of a second office, the owners say, "We're going to add more to this house."

A new lease on life for an outdated ranch house

Even a picturesque country setting in rural northern California didn't brighten the lifeless personality of the 1950s-ranch-style house purchased by architect Obie Bowman and his wife, Helena. "It was a western ranch in gesture only, with decorative wagon wheels and horseshoes, and no character at all," Bowman recalls. Worse, the interior of the 1,500-square-foot house was dark and dismal—thanks to polyurethaned redwood walls that had blackened with age and a minimal number of south-facing windows.

The Bowmans wanted to bring more light to the living spaces, and to create a more gracious entry and a sunny deck area at the front. The plan also included cosmetic changes to help the structure better fit the regional style of the Mendocino coast—a style Bowman describes as "somewhere between tidy New England cottage and stripped-down, economical Victorian farmhouse."

To bring additional light to the interior, the architect pushed a portion of the low-pitched gable roof upward to a height of 16 feet, creating a window-filled tower on the south wall that forms a 12-foot-wide sitting alcove at one end of the living room. He integrated the tower into the exist-

ing design with a shed roof, opening the entire ceiling to the rafters and letting the new portion slope down to meet the old at the ridgeline. The five-sided upper window provides some passive solar benefits during winter months by allowing the sun to penetrate deeply into the room.

Because the budget didn't allow for an all-new entry area, Bowman instead expanded the front porch into a two-tiered deck intended to elongate the entry path and increase the sense of "arrival." The path begins as a concrete walkway that steps up through a latticework trellis onto a

Before the remodeling and expansion of this Northern California ranch-style house, its facade was bland, its south-facing windows small and few, and its interior dark and confining.

An overscaled window seat, 4 feet deep, fits into the sunny alcove at one side of the living room. Custom-ordered $500 windows are worth every penny for their contribution of light. Canvas roll-up shades keep too much sun at bay. Exposed roof truss and deep ledge-top beam mark the original ceiling line.

Multipane kitchen windows frame an attractive view of the surrounding countryside and overlook the multilevel entry deck. Trellis and deck walls were constructed from standard redwood lath, then painted white for a light, airy feel. Skylights in the roof gable extending out over the porch bring more natural light into the kitchen.

redwood deck, then bends and climbs again to meet a sheltered, skylit deck/porch. Combined cost for the tower and deck additions was $16,000.

As finishing touches to their project, the Bowmans painted the house white inside and out, replaced the roof in rust-red composition shingles, and replaced aluminum sliders with wood windows recycled from local buildings.

From the front, this Colonial-style home gives no indication of the 1,500 square feet of south-facing space its owners gained at the rear.

The delicately detailed windows and wide frames were salvaged from the original back wall and repositioned in the master bath and in the third-floor study for continuity.

Colonial front, contemporary back

If you start with a basic two-bedroom, 1932-vintage Colonial house, a small lot, zoning restrictions that forbid any additional height, a desire to retain the home's original character, and a limited budget, how do you gain additional space? This was the challenge facing a Portland, Oregon, couple when they decided they did not want to move away from the area where the husband had grown up, but required additional space for their growing family.

The solution is a perfect blending of the old structure with contemporary design. From the street, there is no evidence that the house has been altered at all. From the rear, it has the look of a modern new home.

The project began with the idea that the second floor could be remodeled and the attic space, with the addition of some dormers, could fill the owners' principal need for a master bedroom/bath suite. But their wish list also included a study and some additional recreational space for their two children, so the owners decided to explore some alternatives.

They took their needs and wish list to three architects who had been recommended by the local chapter of the American Institute of Architects. After looking at portfolios, interviewing each candidate, and visiting some of the projects the designers had completed, they selected Roderick Ashley, a Portland architect who had a number of successful remodel/ addition projects as credits.

They started with a budget of $25,000 to $30,000. The final project, including a 10 percent design fee, licenses, and permits, cost $36,000. Overruns on the construction contract were less than $1,000.

What they got for their money was a 225-square-foot first-floor deck, a new master bedroom/bath suite on the second floor that includes a sitting deck, and a 310-square-foot third-

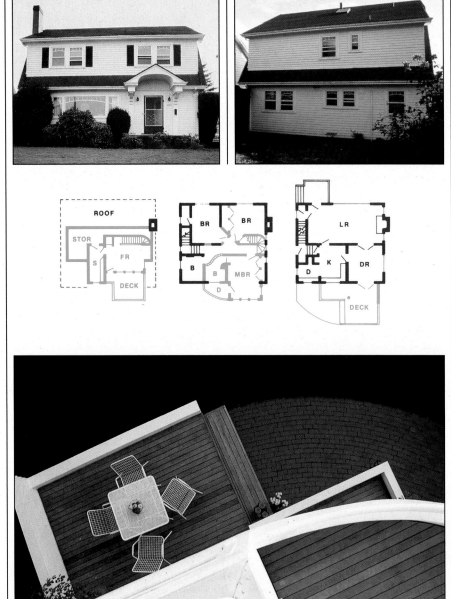

floor recreation room, with a deck that affords a sweeping view of Mt. Hood.

"Beginning with the idea that $25,000 or $30,000 would only remodel the second floor and attic, we were pleasantly surprised that through careful design we could get everything we wanted for only $6,000 more than we had planned," the owners say.

A triple-deck arrangement provides privacy on all levels and encourages the family to spend more time outdoors. Arched detailing of the original windows is reflected in the curves of the second-level master bedroom deck. A partially sheltered cedar entertaining deck on ground level adjoins the dining room.

By bumping out the second floor and raising and flattening part of the peaked attic roof at the rear, the owners gained a master bedroom/bath suite, a television room and study, and private outdoor space.

Ashley provided design options, including the attic remodeling, a separate building with a connecting hallway, and variations of the remodeling/addition that was eventually built. As the final design grew more refined, he also prepared detailed concept drawings and built a model.

Accurately visualizing the final result was important because a zoning variance was required. While the addition did not increase the building's height, its three-story design was in violation of the neighborhood's two-and-a-half-story limit. To ease approval of the variation, Ashley and the homeowners reviewed the drawings and the model with neighbors to be sure there would be no opposition at the public hearing. The variance was granted within six weeks.

The owners originally thought they would act as their own contractor and do most of the work themselves, but finally decided that a professional contractor was required.

Ashley sought bids from four qualified contractors and selected Ground-Up Developers, a small but highly respected Portland firm.

The owners did work with the contractor to develop a schedule of do-it-yourself projects they felt they could handle. They completed demolition with the help of friends and a trash chute and tools provided by the contractor, and they also did some interior and all of the exterior painting.

The addition has been recognized by several national publications and has won design awards, but most importantly the owners say, "we love it. We'd have no qualms about doing it all again."

A mirrored headboard above the bed opens up the master bedroom and forms one wall of the new master bath. The tiled entrance (at right of bed) leads to the bath. The glass-paned door (to left of bed) opens onto a private deck.

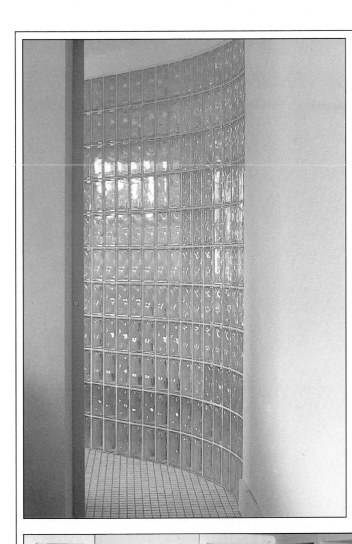

Above left and right: *A glass-block wall lends drama to the master bath, and also lets light flood the second-story hallway. Bright colors on the walls highlight new entries to the existing bedrooms (at left). Entry to the master suite is at end of hall to right.*

Left: *The third-floor television room, which repeats the color scheme of the master bedroom below it, provides 310 square feet of new family living space. A small study and additional storage are through the door at right.*

A detached addition for easy living

Spaciousness, lots of light, fresh air, easy access to the adjoining yard, and plenty of room for family gatherings were the design requirements for this addition to an Alabama home.

The owners, commercial building contractors, gave designer Philip Sides of Sides, McAlpine, Inc. a free hand in developing a solution to meet their needs. What they got was a free-standing addition, connected to the original house by a breezeway that enters into a completely remodeled kitchen.

As a continuation of the original design would have been disruptive, the exterior house design was the principal factor in deciding to move the addition away from the house. While compatible with the old, the new structure is an obvious addition that complements rather than detracts from the main house.

Without the structural restrictions of connecting roof and foundation lines, Sides was able to develop a room that features 14-foot ceilings and floor-to-ceiling window and french door treatments that achieve the roomy, airy atmosphere the owners sought.

The interior furnishings were designed along with the addition. According to Philip Sides, "Every design iteration we looked at included an interior decorating plan of furniture placement and accessories. This procedure allowed us to have a truly complete project when we were done. In fact, we signed off on the project one day and the owners had a large party in the new addition the next night."

E. N. Leary was selected as contractor because of the owners' satisfaction with his performance in constructing the original house. The contract was performed on a cost-plus, fixed-fee basis for approximately $75,000.

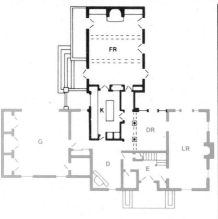

French doors along both long walls, and fixed-pane windows set horizontally above, let plenty of light into this comfortable family-room addition. Crossbraces and area rug separate sitting and dining spaces without formally dividing the room, and partial walls allow easy access to the kitchen. The diagonally laid brick floor gives a rustic feel to the traditionally furnished room.

Above: *A built-in storage wall organizes and displays family treasures beside such everyday items as the television. The lines of the mantel echo the design of the ceiling crossbraces and supports.*

Far left: *The stucco finish of the addition complements the light-toned brick siding of the original house.* **Left:** *A mansard roof overhang shades the lower window.*

Victorian compatibility

The owners' background in art, architecture, and historical preservation is reflected in this addition to a historic Connecticut home.

The couple had already completed the restoration of the Victorian house. Now they wanted to provide a play space for their children that would be accessible to the existing kitchen, but separate enough to avoid disruption and to provide some privacy.

"We wanted a contemporary addition," the owners say. "The design had to be compatible with the original structure, but we felt the addition should reflect the historic evolution of

***Right:** Inside the glass-walled approach to the playroom, color and geometric forms combine to say Welcome. The dramatic ceiling complements the green soffits—punctuated to echo the circular inlays in the room above—which cover and diffuse the lighting.*

***Below:** The gabled roof of a new clapboard-covered playroom above the garage reiterates the lines and scale of this Victorian home's facade and creates an open, airy interior space.*

the house rather than be a reproduction of the original architecture."

The decision to build over the garage was dictated by two practical considerations. A long narrow lot made it difficult to extend any portion of the house; and the desire to maintain the integrity of the original structure ruled out a tacked-on addition.

Selection of the architect, Bernard Wharton of Shope, Reno, Wharton Associates of Greenwich, Connecticut, was done carefully. "It was imperative that this person share our artistic and historical preservation philosophies," the owners say. "But once we had made our choice we gave him the freedom to interpret our ideas and feelings."

The final design retains the sloping rooflines of the original house, and similar materials were used, but be-

yond that no attempt was made to duplicate the existing structure. Transition from the main house to the playroom was accomplished by a glassed-in bridge.

"This was perhaps the single most important element of the design," according to the owners, "because the transition had to be neutral, neither adding to nor detracting from the original house. The glass allows the bridge to almost appear as if it isn't there."

Interior design is contemporary but the window seat, window wells, and bookcase preserve the historic flavor. The high ceiling gives good proportion and a feeling of space to the design. The window seat appears as a bay on the interior, but retains the flat surface on the exterior, another important transitional design feature.

South-facing window illuminates the playroom and dramatically frames the built-in banquette/storage unit. Built-in cases store toys, books, and collectibles, and the easy-to-move furnishings are practically childproof.

The original budget of $65,000, including $10,000 for design, was expanded to $75,000 as the project developed, "mostly because we didn't really know what it might cost at the beginning," the owners admit.

Structurally, the footings of the garage were strong enough to accommodate the second level. Verifying this was the first step taken by the architect. "It was fortunate that was the case," Wharton says, "because to correct it would have been very expensive."

The sill plate was rotted and had to be replaced. This meant raising the garage off its foundation before the start of construction, "an additional expense we had not originally planned for," Wharton says. "However, this was a minor problem compared to the kinds of structural problems we would have faced if we had been adding to the main house."

Wharton managed the project from design through construction and selected the contractor, Olson-Wood Associates, from among candidates who had experience with remodeling and renovating historic structures, and past records of high-quality craftsmanship.

The owners met with Wharton every week to review plans and construction progress. Both sides credit this free flow of frequent communication with aiding the success of the project.

"There were no surprises because we were all aware of everything that was happening as the project evolved," Wharton says.

Because of the historic nature of the community, local zoning ordinances require that neighbors have to approve any additions to existing structures. "We got the neighbors involved early and kept them informed of what we were doing, so getting their approval was not a problem," Wharton says.

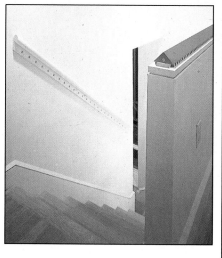

Above: *The north side of the new room consists of two narrow windows and a built-in desk. Skylights permit light to enter from both the east and west sides of the room.*

Left: *Unique design elements—colonnaded building perched atop the stairwell; smaller buildings balancing wood balls at either end of the banquette; and wood insets along stair rail, banquette, and elsewhere throughout the room—add a touch of whimsy to the clean-lined space.*

DESIGNING YOUR ADDITION

The process of designing your addition is actually the development of thought about a physical situation that you want to change. The design process opens your mind to new ways of understanding the space that you already have. The more familiar you are with your house and the possibilities for modifying it, the more opportunities it will present to you.

Before you begin to plan your new addition, be sure you know what you have to work with. In Chapter 2 you surveyed your house, assessing the physical condition of its foundation, structural framework, exterior surfaces, and mechanical systems. In that chapter you also used that information to draw a base plan of your house, a necessary step before you can begin to design your addition.

Planning your addition involves much more than a rough sketch on the back of an envelope. Many professionals say that proper planning represents more than a third of the work to be done in any building or adding-on project. But just because it's difficult, don't try to get by with inadequate planning. As a homeowner you have a tremendous advantage in planning—you have continuous access to your home and you know the kind of activities that go on there. You can test and revise ideas and change your plans accordingly. You can take your time. And you can have a lot of fun.

With the 3-D House Building Kit from Design Works Inc., the PlanAFlex Home Designer, and other design kits available on the market, you can get a preview of how your addition will fit with your existing house. For more information, see page 77.

WHAT DO YOU WANT IN YOUR ADDITION?

I f you feel that step one of the planning process is deciding how to expand the kitchen into the back porch, or where to add the extra bedroom, you're getting ahead of yourself. Back up. Your first task, which could take weeks or even months, is to examine your needs, desires, and motivations for wanting to add on to your house in the first place.

Ask yourself this question: What should our home look like in five years? The idea is to see in larger perspective what you and your family really want for your home. Then you can form long-range goals and design an addition that best meets those goals.

How do the members of your household go about discovering their wants and needs and setting goals? The best way is to make lists. Start a notebook. You'll come back to it time and again. Your initial lists don't have to be well written, logical, or even practical. It's important to include everyone in your family, even future members.

Sit down together and list what you want for your home. You can use the list of questions in the box on this page to stimulate your thinking. Be sure to note your desires as well as your needs, since extravagant fantasies don't cost anything at this stage. There's plenty of time to be practical later. Simply write down what comes to mind. For example:
☐ More storage, especially for sheets and towels
☐ A greenhouse window in the kitchen
☐ A fireplace
☐ Somewhere for the kids to play
☐ A family feeling of warmth and togetherness
☐ A larger dining area
☐ A quiet place to study
☐ A bright and sunny feeling
☐ Secret and private spaces
☐ More room for guests
☐ A television room where the TV can't be heard from the kitchen

Also list the underlying reasons for each idea. Why do you want to make a change? Do you need more space, want a more modern look, or intend to make your house more energy efficient?

After everyone has had a chance to offer ideas, pool them together. You will have dozens of suggestions and dozens of reasons for them. After some refining, you will have a tool to use in the next step, which is to establish a list of concrete goals. These goals may change over the coming weeks and months, but for now continue to add to your list as new ideas occur to you. Try to identify the underlying reasons that overlap and build on each other.

These reasons and their suggestions will help generate some specific goals for your home addition. For example:
☐ A kitchen where the family can come together
☐ A walk-in closet so the new downstairs bathroom won't feel messy and cluttered
☐ A dining room for formal and elegant entertaining
☐ An attractive facade and entry to make guests feel welcome
☐ An upstairs master suite with an intimate, private feeling
☐ A sunny breakfast nook to make it easier to get going in the morning
☐ A basement recreation room where the children can play without getting underfoot

Reasons are important because they can help bring agreement over differences later on, they can help you see other ways to accomplish the same goals, and they can help you set priorities.

Questions to ask yourself about your addition

Once you have completed your base plan and made all the necessary notations, ask yourself and your family the following questions. The answers will help you evaluate your family's needs.

1. What uses do you currently make of the various areas in your existing house?

2. What do you most like about your house?

3. What don't you like about it?

4. How do you and other members of your family plan to use the new spaces?

5. If you have children, what specific uses will they be growing into and out of?

6. If you have pets, do they have any specific requirements that will influence your design?

7. What is the architectural style of your house? What aspects of it do you want to carry through into your addition?

8. How much money have you budgeted for your addition?

9. How much time will you have to devote to the project?

10. Are the materials you want to use easily available? Are there any materials or objects you want to use to create a special feeling?

11. Are there any easements, setbacks, or other zoning regulations that will influence what you can add?

12. Are there any underground utility lines or old water pipes you need to take into account in planning your addition?

13. Are you aware of any other considerations that will influence the planning and construction of your addition?

Even if you aren't able to give complete answers, keep these questions in mind as you work into the concept-drawing phase of your planning. Knowing what you *don't* know can help you be on the lookout for the answers.

ROOM-BY-ROOM PLANNING

T he house inspection and base plan you completed in Chapter 2 provided new information for revising and refining your goals, made you more aware of your home's construction and all the features you want to preserve, and showed you any limitations that might prevent a particular type of addition.

Once you've established your long-range goals, the next step is design. Design is probably the single most important aspect of your addition, so important that it can easily determine the success or failure of your project. Many people associate the word *design* with style and decoration. But in the context of planning an addition, it means much more. It means an overall plan that offers the best solution to problems presented by the situation at hand. Design decisions involve intangibles. Often there is no one right answer; any problem may have a number of good workable solutions.

In planning your addition, whether it's a simple bump-out, a single room, or a whole wing, common sense often determines the most appropriate use of space. Your experience and house inspection notes will also guide you. Here are some overall guidelines to remember.

□ *Consider key activity centers.* Some rooms serve a single function, while others may have several uses. Imagine how your household members might use each new room you're thinking of adding—for conversation, reading, game playing, television viewing, sleeping, and so forth. Also consider where guests tend to gather.

□ *What is the physical space like?* Will the room you're planning be large enough for its intended purpose? Will it be too large? If it's too large, it may present visual and auditory problems. What is the shape of the room? Are the proportions pleasing? In general it's best to keep room shapes simple for effective use of space and low construction costs.

□ *How does the new space work with the old?* As you plan your addition, pay special attention to the way the new and the old spaces fit together. Will the addition have a separate entrance? If not, how will access to the new space affect traffic patterns? Will any of the existing space have to be remodeled?

□ *Traffic patterns and circulation.* Traffic flow and circulation are a major consideration in room layouts. Although areas must be separated, they need to be properly related as well. Circulation provides the key to a good floor plan.

□ *Don't overlook details.* Minor details can make a big difference in how a room works. As you work on your plan, consider these points: Do the doors swing the right way? Will they cause awkward disruptions? You may have planned enough light switches and electrical outlets, but will they be accessible once the room is furnished? Will closet space and storage be adequate? Are several furniture arrangements possible?

□ *Do you have enough light and ventilation?* Would a skylight or more windows help? Will the artificial lighting be adequate? Even if you have air-conditioning, each room should have natural ventilation as well.

□ *Can you improve energy efficiency?* Will your addition face south for heat gain in colder areas? Will trees shade the windows? Will ceiling height and expansive window areas affect heat loss?

Designing with kits

Design kits can add to the fun of planning your addition. Their scaled grids and shapes let you try out a variety of arrangements to visualize scale, placement, and traffic flow.

With the 3-D House Building Kit from Design Works Inc. (11 Hitching Post Rd., Amherst, MA 01002; 413/549-4763) you can build a scale model of your house and its proposed addition. The kit contains printed cardboard sheets that mimic sidings, roofing materials, and floor coverings, as well as landscape elements for a complete picture. The Architect's Drawing Kit provides premarked grids for making perspective drawings from various angles. For the interior, 2-D kits drawn in perspective include about 80 shapes representing furniture, or kitchen appliances and bathroom fixtures, or architectural elements such as windows and doors. The plastic shapes stick to a treated grid board large enough to lay out one room.

Plan-It-Kit Inc. (Box 429, Westport, CT 06881; 203/259-8896) concentrates on interior design aids. Its 3-D kit includes styrene furniture in ½-inch scale, a 1,200-square-foot grid, and "walls" to which you can attach doors and windows. It's very useful for visualizing height relationships. The 2-D kit contains about 80 cardboard furniture templates with dimensions printed on them, and a slightly smaller grid board.

The PlanAFlex Design series from Procreations Publishing Co. (8129 Earhart Blvd., New Orleans, LA 70118; 800/245-8779) includes whole-house, landscape, kitchen, and bath kits composed of plastic grid sheets and die-cut plastic design elements. The Home Designer contains about 500 colored templates, with printed dimensions, for furnishings.

Kitchens

If you plan to add on a new kitchen, or to expand your old one, first consider the overall purpose you want it to serve. Is it to be a work center only? Or do you need a multipurpose room for dining and family activities? Second, decide which type of eating arrangement you prefer. Do you want a breakfast nook, a serving counter, an alcove, or a separate dining room? Third, arrange the various activity centers to provide the most efficient kitchen plan.

Every kitchen has three main activity centers.

☐ The food storage center includes the refrigerator/freezer, cabinets, and counter space.

☐ The cooking center includes a range or cooktop, oven, counter space on either side, ventilating equipment, and cabinets and drawers for utensils.

☐ The cleanup center includes the sink, counter space on either side, a garbage disposal, a dishwasher, and a trash compactor.

The efficient arrangement of these three centers is called a *work triangle*. The most common layouts are illustrated here.

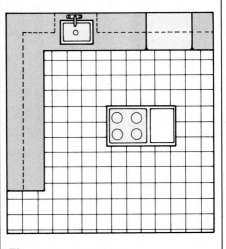

*The **L-shaped kitchen** eliminates through traffic, and can create an eating area adjacent to the work triangle.*

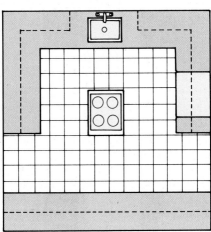

*The **U-shaped kitchen** is generally considered the most desirable. It offers continuous counter area and the shortest walking distance between appliances. The **island kitchen**, a modified U or L shape, is a good plan for two people who like to cook together. If the island is used as a cooking center, however, venting can be a problem.*

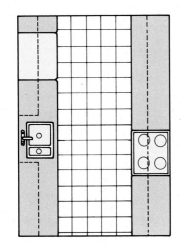

*The **corridor kitchen** is the simplest and often the most economical arrangement. The corridor should be at least 4 feet wide to allow traffic to pass, but the kitchen location should not encourage through traffic.*

*The **one-wall kitchen** is the least desirable layout, but may be necessary in some situations. If it is, the sink should be in the center of the work flow. The overall length of the kitchen wall should be no more than 13 feet.*

The location of each activity center determines the efficiency of the kitchen. For example, the range should not be located next to the refrigerator. Nor should the range be located directly under a window. Breezes may interfere with gas burners, and curtains can catch fire. The local code may determine the location of the range for venting and safety, so check on this. The sink is best located under a window for natural light and a view. The dishwasher should be within 12 inches of the sink, placed so that its door does not block traffic.

As you plan, keep the following dimensions in mind.

☐ For efficiency the overall size of the kitchen should be not more than 160 square feet.

☐ Distances recommended by efficiency experts for the three sides of the work triangle are: 4 to 7 feet from the sink to the refrigerator, 4 to 6 feet from the sink to the range, and 4 to 9 feet from the range to the refrigerator. This means that no two basic appliances should be less than 4 feet apart.

☐ The total perimeter of the work triangle should be 12 to 22 feet.

☐ Allow 15 to 18 inches of counter space on the latch side of the refrigerator for loading and unloading.

☐ Allow 30 to 36 inches of counter space on both sides of the sink.

☐ Allow at least 24 inches of counter space on both sides of the range; 30 inches is preferable.

☐ Countertops are normally 24 inches deep and 32 to 36 inches high, depending on personal preference and comfort.

☐ For specific appliance and cabinet sizes, measure your existing units carefully or take new dimensions from manufacturers' catalogs and data sheets. Be sure to allow sufficient space for doors to swing open completely.

For more information and ideas about kitchen planning, see Ortho's book *How to Design and Remodel Kitchens.*

Bathrooms

First, consider the overall function of the bath you want to add. Will it be a half-bath with a washbasin and toilet, or a full family bath? Do you want to include a dressing area or laundry equipment? What about extras such as a sauna or steam bath? Will the bath be used by all family members?

Economy is an important consideration in deciding on location and layout. Use existing plumbing lines whenever possible. This means a back-to-back arrangement with another bath or kitchen, or an upstairs bath located over the first-floor plumbing connections.

The layout of the principal fixtures can be a U-shaped, L-shaped, or corridor arrangement. If you live in a cold climate, locate the water supply and drain-waste-vent lines in an interior wall to prevent freezing. Avoid a layout that allows a door to swing into any fixture. Don't locate the tub under a window. Cold drafts can be uncomfortable, and the window is more difficult to open with the tub in the way. The best tub layout is enclosed by three walls or an alcove.

Several dimensions are specified by the plumbing code; check your local code for additional spacing.

☐ Generally a full bathroom requires a space at least 5 by 7 feet.

☐ The thickness of the wet wall that conceals the drains and soil stack may need to be 2 by 6 inches rather than 2 by 4.

☐ Allow a minimum of 24 inches from the front rim of a toilet to a facing wall.

☐ Allow 18 inches from the center line of the toilet to an adjacent wall and 15 inches to an adjacent fixture.

☐ The minimum size for a shower stall is 32 by 32 inches.

For specific fixture sizes, measure the existing fixtures carefully or take new dimensions from manufacturers' catalogs and data sheets. For more information and ideas on planning a bathroom, see Ortho's book *How to Design and Remodel Bathrooms.*

L-shaped

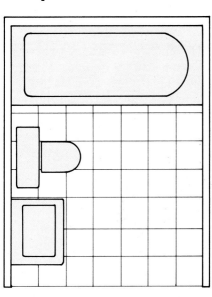

Corridor

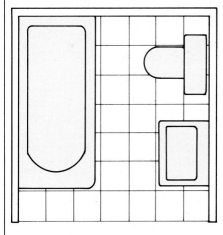

U-shaped

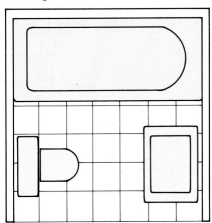

Dining areas

For obvious reasons, the dining area should be located near the kitchen. The dining area need not be a separate room. Although there are advantages to screening the dining area from the kitchen, an alcove that is part of the kitchen or living room saves space and allows for multiple traffic patterns.

In making your plan, consider these key dimensions.

☐ To seat eight people comfortably, you'll need an area approximately 12 by 15 feet.

☐ Allow at least 24 inches of table space for each place setting; 30 inches is better.

☐ Allow at least 36 inches from the edge of the table to a nearby wall to provide adequate space for seating and rising.

Living rooms

The typical living room serves several functions with a single furniture arrangement. Design your new living room to accommodate all the activities that will be going on in the room.

Plan your room arrangement for maximum flexibility. You'll need to have access to several activity areas at the same time. Avoid plans that require rearranging furniture every time you want to play a game or watch TV.

Dining area

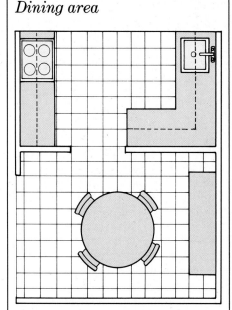

Traffic patterns are critical. The number of entry/exits to the living room should be kept to a minimum. To protect the living room, an entrance hall or foyer should provide direct access to other rooms of the house.

The following dimensions will affect your planning.

☐ Although it's difficult to give a minimum size, 12 by 18 feet is considered a small to modest size for a living room.

☐ The maximum distance that allows a comfortable arc of conversation is between 6 and 8 feet.

Bedrooms

First, consider the different activity areas and functions of the bedroom(s) you plan to add. The needs for a master bedroom are obviously different than for a child's room. For instance, a master bedroom may include sitting and dressing areas, walk-in closets, and a private deck.

Unless you have a family room or a playroom, you may want to provide extra play space in a child's bedroom. Teenagers will need a place to study, including a desk, comfortable chair, and good lighting. You might build loft beds that create usable space underneath.

Because of drafts, beds should not be located under a window. One wall of the bedroom should be free of doors and windows to allow for the bed. Plan sufficient space on either side of the bed to accommodate a bedside table, and to make it easy to make up the bed.

Here are some key dimensions.

☐ The minimum bedroom size is usually 70 square feet, but check your local code on this.

☐ Allow at least 22 inches from the edge of the bed to an adjacent wall or closet for room to make the bed.

☐ Allow at least 40 inches in front of a dresser or bureau to provide access to all the drawers.

☐ Allow at least 36 inches in front of a closet to provide access and room for dressing and grooming.

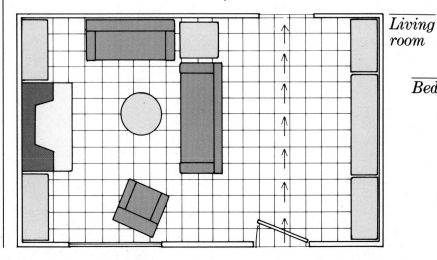

Living room

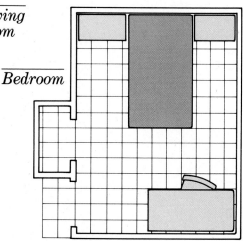

Bedroom

THE DESIGN PROCESS

The preceding design suggestions, together with your house inspection and long-term goal list, give you the information you need to start the actual design of your addition. Design is both a process and an end product. The design process is a series of techniques used to create new ideas and to define the project.

The end product of this process is a finished design. Its first stage is a *concept plan,* which shows the general arrangement of space and how different elements of the design relate to one another. A working plan takes the concept plan to its conclusion, showing the exact sizes, shapes, and materials to be used. The *working plan,* usually in blueprint form, is used by the building department and contractors for permits, estimates, and actual construction.

This section will show you how to develop a concept plan for your addition. The techniques used in the design process are divided into three stages: research, create, and critique. During the design process you will go back and forth between these phases in a continuing cycle.

Research. This is the preliminary stage of all design. Research is simply a matter of gathering all the information you can find that pertains to your particular addition needs. There are many sources to which you can turn.

□ *Magazines.* "Shelter" publications, which deal with the home and its design, are full of innovative plans and new ways to use materials and products. The ads will keep you informed about the newest and best of the products currently on the market.

□ *Trade publications.* If you have access to a large public library or the office of an architect or contractor, look over some of the magazines distributed only to the trade. Some manufacturers, such as hardware producers, advertise only to the trade, and you will not get to see their products anywhere else.

□ *Manufacturers.* In most ads, the manufacturer provides some method for obtaining further information. This information includes brochures, many of them in color; specification sheets that give actual dimensions and finishes for the various lines of products; pamphlets that instruct you on how to install certain elements; and lists of dealers in your area.

□ *Professional and trade associations.* Manufacturers and professionals belong to associations that often provide lists of local dealer sources and materials. They may also produce informative booklets. Most will not recommend individual manufacturers, suppliers, or design professionals, but they can be helpful in answering your general questions.

□ *Showrooms and home shows.* One of the best ways to get hands-on knowledge about specific products that intrigue you is to visit the showrooms of kitchen, bathroom, and bedroom specialists; building suppliers; plumbing suppliers; lumberyards; home improvement centers; and home shows. Although some outlets sell only to contractors and other professionals, you can still inspect an array of products, with specifications, that you might not find elsewhere.

□ *Your notebook.* You will quickly accumulate a pile of materials that you should organize to maintain a sense of order during your planning. File folders, scrapbooks, and three-ring binders with pockets are all helpful for grouping brochures, magazine pages, and notes. Separate them under such headings as Layout, Kitchen, Office, Appliances, Lighting, and so on. As you sort your papers into categories, the whirl of ideas circling around in your mind will also begin to sort itself out.

Clip photos from brochures rather than keeping piles of dog-eared pamphlets. Make a note of any dimensions necessary for planning, and put pamphlets dealing with installation aside during the planning stage.

Create. In this second phase, all the research you've assembled, including the base plan of your house, is put to use. Some of this information has an obvious, direct application to your project. Much of your research, however, is only raw material that you as the designer will transform into something totally new. Your creativity will develop new ideas and new solutions. Some of these ideas will be good, some not so good, but in this part of the process that doesn't matter. The essential task is to create as many different ideas, sketches, and plans as possible.

Critique. In this final stage, you evaluate the ideas and plans generated in phase two. This involves a conscious sorting and selecting process. You discard poor ideas and refine those that show some promise. In phase two your thinking is imaginative, fanciful, and free-wheeling; in phase three it is conservative, rational, and pragmatic. In combination, these two stages of the design process provide a natural check and balance.

Is it time to hire a designer?

If you plan a major addition to your house, or if you're not entirely certain of what you want, you should definitely consider hiring a professional designer—an architect, building designer, or draftsman. (For a discussion of the skills of these professionals, see page 88.) The many advantages of hiring a professional far outweigh the cost of the services. The designer's experience can pay off in several ways: saving money on materials; simplifying construction procedures; preparing contract materials for the contractor; making sure the project meets local codes and zoning ordinances; preparing working drawings; and most importantly, creating an efficient and pleasing arrangement.

Too often the first cost-cutting move in an adding-on project is to dispense with the designer's services. In many instances this is a serious mistake. The designer's responsibility is to provide the best possible design for the amount of money you have to spend. Even if you prefer to handle the design yourself, you should have a professional designer review your concept plan. A few simple changes or suggestions at this point could save you hundreds of dollars and a lot of disappointment in the future.

Concept drawings

Concept drawings illustrate every aspect of your planning and design process, from the most formless of notions to the detailed drawings on which blueprints are based.

The bubble plan

Your first plans of your addition should be rough sketches, even doodles, that merely show spaces and zones in relation to each other. From your list of goals and needs, you will probably see certain groupings emerge. Represent these on paper with bubbles, linking them to each other where there should be a passageway or flow of space. Don't worry about scale, shape, or detail.

The purpose of the concept drawing is to figure out solutions to your particular needs for additional space. Use a concept drawing to get an idea of how you want one space to relate to another; the size of the rooms; the connections and circulation between the new spaces and the old; and special design considerations, such as sequences and the separation of public and private spaces. Concentrate on how you will use and move around within the spaces and what form the space will take. Remember that there are usually many good solutions to any design problem, not just one.

At this point you are seeing how various functions relate to each other in terms of the space they occupy in your home. For instance, areas for eating and areas for preparing food should be close to each other, if not connected. Do you also want them to be connected to an entertaining area? Do you want eating areas close to sleeping areas? How do the sleeping areas relate to entertaining areas? Where should working areas be?

Experiment with many different arrangements—tracing paper is cheap. As you arrange and draw your preliminary concept designs, keep in mind that you are creating space for activities—studying, eating, relaxing, socializing, sleeping. Think of the real or ideal connections between these spaces, such as easy access from the dining room to the kitchen, or from the laundry area to the bedroom or bathroom. Pay particular attention to circulation—the effective use of any room is reduced if it becomes simply a corridor from one place to another.

Draw sketch after sketch on tracing paper, saving only those that seem to have the best points. Most of all, be conscious of the basic form—the bubbles of space—and how well various designs create continuity and flow, and answer your needs. This is the time to experiment with a variety of forms for the spaces you want to add to your house. You can lay out rectangles, squares, circles, angles, and free forms in many sizes and configurations, each on a separate overlay, to see whether they appeal to you or not. During the concept phase, limit your attention to general uses and structural considerations. Later on, during the working-drawing phase, you can refine your plan and select actual materials and dimensions.

At some point you will need to merge these bubble diagrams with the floor plan of your existing house. One way is to draw the floor plan as a bubble diagram and see how it meshes with your experimental plans. You may see a way to alter a few spaces to accommodate all your needs and wants; or you may have to consider an extensive addition.

Refining the concept drawing

Your next step is to convert the bubble diagram into a more refined representation of spaces. Now the size, shape, location, and relationship of these spaces becomes more important. You must take into consideration the dimensions of existing rooms that will remain intact, the condition of the house, and environmental factors like views and sunlight.

Use graph paper to speed the measuring process. Then use tracing paper to refine ideas by duplicating

Bubble plan

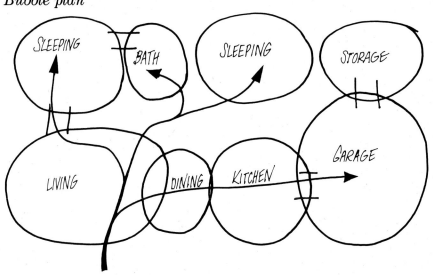

only certain rooms or sections and trying out variations for adjacent areas.

Keep playing with various ideas, spaces, and sketches. For example, you might turn a sketch upside down and ask yourself, "What if we did this?" Or you might remove all the labels from your plan and switch rooms around to see what happens. Just because a room is designated as a laundry room or a bedroom doesn't mean it can't serve another function as well. Some of your most creative ideas will emerge from this kind of playful attitude. The design process is a cycle that takes time; don't expect to design everything in one sitting.

Gradually you'll refine your ideas to the point where one or more concepts show possibilities. Now is the time to begin incorporating dimensions and standard lumber sizes. Many building materials come in 4- by 8-foot panels; lumber is sold in 2-foot increments. Plan to use these standard sizes in your design. It's fine if your plans remain rough at this stage of the design, but eventually you should provide as much detail as you can.

Once you've settled on an interior floor plan, it's time to think about how the addition will affect the exterior of your house. Start by making rough sketches of the existing exterior, then show with dotted lines or a second color how the addition will appear from all sides. Use the illustrations on pages 8–9 as a guide. Pay particular attention to the appearance of the new roofline in conjunction with the old, and to the places where the addition meets the existing house. Chapter 3 outlines the most common exterior design problems to watch for, and their solutions.

Testing your plans

Review the key dimensions in the section on design basics to be sure you've allowed minimum spacing. You should also trace the traffic patterns on a separate overlay to see if the circulation is efficient.

Determine if your concept plan for your addition really meshes with your needs and goals. If it doesn't, refine the plan until all your requirements are satisfied. Don't compromise your goals just because you haven't found a solution yet. Keep sketching and refining until you do.

After you have created one or more concept plans that seem right, there are several techniques you can use to test them. Each of these ideas can help you visualize your plans more easily and possibly point out flaws and problems.

A walk-through. In your mind's eye simply imagine yourself walking through your plan from one end to the other. Pay particular attention to the circulation patterns between the existing house and the addition. Reverse directions and walk through the space again. Concentrate on imagining yourself in each part of the addition. Imagine each member of the family doing the same. Ask other members of your household to look over your plan and imagine themselves walking through it.

Interior elevations. If you are having trouble visualizing certain aspects of your design, doing a scale drawing of each room's walls is useful for seeing how things fit, and for selecting finish materials.

Scale models. Take the template concept into three dimensions. Use cardboard or balsa wood from a hobby shop to construct a model of your addition. Don't worry about details or exact sizes—it's the overall space that's important. Scale models range from the simple to the sophisticated. A hobby shop or your local library will have books of detailed instructions for their construction.

Slides. Take several slides of the exterior of your house and project them onto drawing paper. Use the projected house to trace your old house and sketch in the form of the addition. (You can also use snapshots blown up to 4 by 5 or 8 by 10 inches.) This will help you visualize the size of the addition in proportion to the existing house.

Stakes and string. Set up stakes in the ground at the outlines of the proposed addition and stretch strings between them to show the outlines of the rooms.

The working drawings

Your concept plans show the general arrangement of spaces in your existing house and in your proposed addition, and how all of the different elements of the design relate to one another. The dimensions may be only approximate. Before you can proceed with your project, you need to develop a set of *working drawings.* A working drawing is an accurate, scaled rendition of your final concept drawing. Working drawings are so called because the information on them alone should be sufficient to allow a contractor to build your addition.

A working drawing indicates graphically what kind, what size, and how many of each item you will need to complete the project. It also shows how to put the materials together. You may be able to draw these plans yourself, or you may want to hire a professional to do it for you.

First find out if the local code requires working plans to be professionally drawn and if any structural elements require engineering analysis. If so, you will have to contact an engineer, designer, or draftsman to provide these services. If your local building department does permit you to draw your own plans, be sure to determine how detailed they must be.

Even if you hire a professional designer to draw up your working plans, you should provide him or her with the most complete drawings you can, including room dimensions and specifications for materials. Step-by-step instructions for drawing working plans are beyond the scope of this book. To learn the proper symbols and procedures you can use a drafting text such as *Drafting: Tips and Tricks of the Trade* by Bob Syvanen (East Woods Press, 1981).

FOUR ADDITIONS TO THE BASIC HOUSE PLAN

L-shaped addition

A small wing added to this basic house contains a new master bedroom and large bath with a hot tub/spa. Remodeling of the original second bedroom and bath was necessary to allow access to the new wing. Bubble plans for each addition illustrated here show traffic circulation patterns throughout the original house and the addition.

L-shaped addition

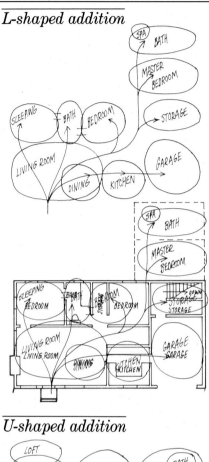

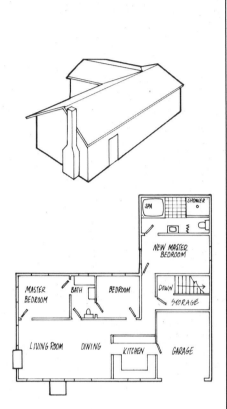

U-shaped addition

With the addition of two wings, the basic house gains three new living areas: a spacious guest bedroom with bath; a private study with a loft accessible by a spiral staircase; and a secluded patio that can be reached from both new wings as well as from the second bedroom in the original house. As in the L-shaped addition, remodeling of the original second bedroom and bath was necessary.

U-shaped addition

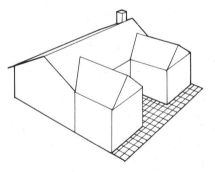

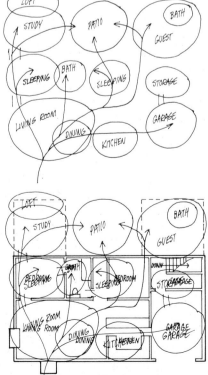

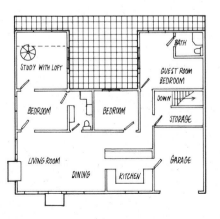

Small second-story addition

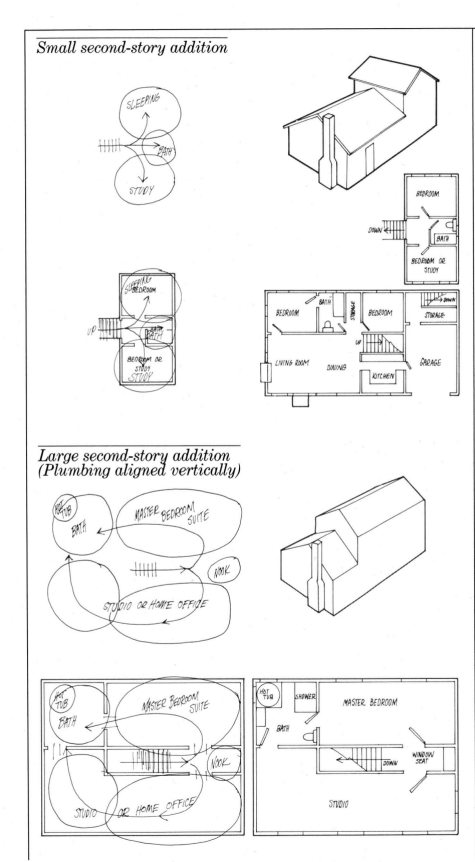

Large second-story addition
(Plumbing aligned vertically)

Partial second story

This small second story, placed over the garage and storage area, is compact but efficient, adding a second bath, a guest bedroom, and either a fourth bedroom or a study. Stairs fill the original storage area.

Large second story

This second-story addition is set back 10 feet 1 inch from the chimney. A cozy window seat area leads into a new master bedroom, complete with hot tub/spa, and into a spacious studio or home office. In fact, the studio is so large that it could be divided into a guest bedroom and a small study. Plumbing is vertically aligned from the addition to the existing bathroom.

MANAGING AND FINANCING YOUR PROJECT

I*n the last chapter you learned about the step-by-step process of designing your addition. It's quite possible, however, that you won't want to draw up any plans beyond the very roughest sketches. In that case you would hire a design professional to work with you on developing your ideas of what you want and need in your addition, and ultimately to provide working drawings. In fact, you should be able to contract for any portion of the professional's services, from advice about zoning laws to the full spectrum from concept to working drawings. In this chapter you will find descriptions of design professionals, the kinds of services they normally provide, and a step-by-step guide to interviewing and selecting the individual or firm that will give you the results you want.*

The owners of this Connecticut beach house attribute much of the success of their family room addition to the team of professionals with whom they worked. "We had a fine architect who paid close attention to detail and a good contractor who earned our total trust," they say. For more information, see pages 54-55.

WORKING WITH DESIGN PROFESSIONALS

Whoever does the work, your goals for your project will be the same. You want a design that suits your taste; is structurally suited to your house and lot; includes plans and specifications that are complete and correct; and can be built within your budget. Keeping these goals firmly in mind will help you in your selection of a design professional.

Architects. Architects are trained specifically for building design and engineering, and some offer consulting services for do-it-yourselfers. In order to be licensed, an architect must complete five to eight years of architectural training, followed by a three-year apprenticeship, and then pass a state licensing exam. The initials *AIA* after an architect's name designate membership in the American Institute of Architects, a professional association for advancing the practice of architecture. Membership in the AIA is voluntary, and its lack is not a reflection of an architect's competence.

The architect who specializes in adding on can offer you three important services.

☐ *Design services.* After discussing your goals and needs for your addition, the architect will create several concept plans. He or she will show you sketches and floor plans to help you visualize the ideas and will revise these plans until you find a solution that satisfies your particular requirements. The architect will also help you to estimate costs and to make the design financially feasible.

☐ *Working plans and specifications.* Once the design is finalized, the architect can produce a set of finished plans and specifications for you to submit to the building department, contractors, and subcontractors.

☐ *Supervision.* If you choose, the architect will supervise your entire project, including suggesting various contractors, sending the plans out for bids, and inspecting the progress of the work regularly.

Other types of professionals offer many of the same services as an architect. You may hire them for design, working drawings, supervision, or all three. The method of payment, either by fee or on an hourly basis, is also similar.

Building designers. The training of building designers is often similar to that of architects. In most states the American Institute of Building Designers offers the *AIBD* designation to designers who have at least three years of architectural or building technology training, three years of experience, requisite letters of recommendation, and have passed stringent testing. In many states, the services provided are very similar to those offered by architects.

Design/build contractors. Design/build contractors accept full responsibility for a project from design through construction. The firm may employ architects or designers, or may subcontract for such services. These firms offer full legal responsibility and accountability from the beginning to the end of a project. Contractors must be licensed in most states. When considering a design/build firm, make sure the professionals you will be working with have the specific design or construction expertise your project requires.

Draftsmen. The draftsman has the training and ability to take rough sketches of your ideas and draw up a complete set of working plans and specifications. He or she may offer limited design services, although these are primarily technical and not conceptual. The draftsman does not inspect or oversee construction.

Interior designers and decorators. Interior designers are concerned with such matters as traffic flow, lighting, and anything having to do with how the space is to be used. Interior decorators are concerned with fixtures and accessories, colors, types of window treatments, furnishings, and anything else having to do with appearance. Either of these professionals may provide advice in conjunction with an architect or designer.

If you plan to use an interior designer or decorator, tell your architect at the beginning. They may be able to suggest someone with whom they have worked before. It is important for these professionals to communicate well and have respect for one another, as their decisions have to be coordinated and combined in the final design.

How to find a design professional

How do you go about locating the architect or building designer who will design the space that's right for you, who will stay within your budget, and who will inspire your continuing confidence? Listed below are several possible starting points.

☐ *Ask friends.* One of the best ways to find a professional you can trust is to ask friends, relatives, or neighbors to recommend people they have worked with.

☐ *Use the Yellow Pages.* Check the Yellow Pages and your local newspaper for advertisements. Architects rarely advertise, but they do take Yellow Page listings, which often mention their specialties.

☐ *Consult trade associations.* Call the local chapter of the American Institute of Architects, the National Association of Home Builders, and the American Institute of Building Designers for recommendations of people who work in your area and who specialize in the type of project you have in mind.

☐ *Attend trade shows.* The annual home shows and remodeling and decorating shows that are held in most communities are another good source. These events offer you the opportunity to meet and talk with professionals without having to make a commitment.

☐ *Consult a profit-making referral service.* These services recommend firms from among their subscribers. The referral costs you nothing; the subscriber pays for the leads received.

☐ *Drive around.* A less scientific but often rewarding method is to drive around the community looking for construction projects that are similar to what you want. Stop and ask who is doing the work. Most people will be glad to help, and pleased that you stopped.

☐ *Visit home improvement centers and lumberyards.* These stores often have a bulletin board for tradespeople to leave their business cards.

The first contact

When you have collected the names of several people or firms that may be able to do your work, you can make your first contact by phone, in order to narrow the list to two or three you will want to interview in person.

Take notes from each conversation so that your first reactions will be recorded and you will have an accurate account of who said what. The box at right gives a list of suggested questions to ask at this stage. In this initial contact you should provide a general idea of what you have in mind (a new second story, a new wing, etc.), some idea of your total budget, and when you would like the addition to be completed. No more detail than that should be required for your first contact. During this conversation you will be primarily looking for:

☐ *Responsiveness.* Did you get someone on the phone promptly who could give you the information you wanted?

☐ *Respect.* Were you treated with patience and courtesy?

☐ *Availability.* Does the firm do the kind of work you want? Can they do it in the time frame you require? Do they normally work in your area?

☐ *References.* Are they willing and able to give names and addresses of people for whom they have done jobs similar to the one you are planning?

Selecting design professionals

Questions to ask on the phone

Are you interested in the addition project we have described?
Is our neighborhood within your normal work area?
Would you be able to handle the project within the time schedule we have outlined?
Are you licensed?
How long have you been licensed?
Have you been licensed under a different name? If you have been licensed under a different name, why did you change?
Will you provide trade, credit, and bank references?
Will you provide references from jobs that are similar in scope to what we are considering? (If so, get names, addresses, and telephone numbers.)
May we visit the job sites?
Do you handle the complete design phase?
Do you use a licensed architect, certified designer, or other for a project like this?
Were the jobs you referenced designed by the same person who would handle our project?

Questions to ask in an interview

What information will you need from us, and how many times will we have to meet before a design is complete?
What assurance can you give us that your design will be within our budget?
What percentage of the projects designed by your firm actually get built?
Do you work with a schedule that shows target completion dates for each major phase of design?
Could you describe for us your basic design philosophy and how you will work to achieve a design that is pleasing to us?
What provisions does your design contract include? (For more information, see "What a design contract should include," page 91.)
Will you provide us with a sample of the contract you propose to use?
After the design is complete, how do you proceed?
Will you assist with bidding or negotiation for a contractor?
How do you handle construction supervision?
How much responsibility do you take for the construction phase?
Does your firm help with financing arrangements?
What are your trade, credit, and bank references?

Questions to ask references

Who specifically did the design work?
Who coordinated the project?
Who did the construction?
Were you happy with the project?
Was the designer responsive to your requests, creative in suggesting alternate approaches, and sensitive to your budget limitations?
How much variance was there between the preliminary cost estimate and the final cost?
What caused these gaps between estimates and final cost?
Did you experience any significant surprises that affected cost or schedule of the project?
Was construction completed on time and within budget?
Would you recommend that we consider using your designer for our project?
Do you have any suggestions that would help us work well with this person or firm?

Following up the first contact

References are extremely important. Be sure to check them; don't just talk to them on the phone. And don't settle for looking at pictures. The only way you can assess whether a firm is likely to perform the kind of work you want is to see something they have already done, and to talk with the people for whom they worked.

When you visit the references, be thorough in your inspection. Be mindful of such details as quality of workmanship, as well as the overall feeling of the place. Take along a notebook to record your on-the-spot impressions and the answers to specific questions you may have about the work.

Making your selection

After making calls and checking references, you should be able to narrow the field to two or three individuals or firms that impress you. These are the ones you want to meet with in person. Follow-up interviews may be conducted either at your home or at the professional's office. Be prepared to provide as much information as possible about what you want to do. Bring your sketches, examples, product brochures, and so forth to the meeting. And be prepared as well to discuss your budget and plans for financing your project. There's no point in withholding information; your ability to select someone depends partly on how they react to the information you provide.

In this interview, as well as answering the professional's questions, be sure you also get the information you need (see the box on page 89). Although the architect or designer will know more about how to build an addition than you do, don't feel intimidated. It's your home, and you're the one who knows what you want in your addition.

Evaluating professionals

If you have followed the selection procedures outlined above, all of your candidates should be capable of producing the kind of work you want. Therefore, the one you like best, are most comfortable with, and trust the most is the proper choice. In making your evaluation, keep the following points in mind.

☐ Ask yourself, does this person think the way I do? Do we share the same philosophy? Does this person like the same things I do? Will I be comfortable entrusting my home to this person? Will I enjoy working with him or her? Can he or she be creative within my budget limitations? Can I trust this person to go to bat for me if things go wrong? Is he or she careful and thorough in all details?

☐ Each professional you interview should prepare a proposal that spells out a specific course of action; the charges for specific tasks and the total estimated design cost; the time each phase will take; and at least a rough idea of the basic approach they have in mind, such as a new wing or a second story.

Once you make your selection, you will be ready to develop a contract with the firm or individual.

Contracting for design

Regardless of the type of design professional you choose, you will be making two contracts: one for the design-to-construction phases and one for construction. Construction and construction management are not covered in depth in this book, but you will need to consider these when selecting a design professional.

If you choose an architect or building designer, you will probably want him or her to participate in the bidding and negotiation with contractors and supervision of construction, unless you are sure you have the time and expertise to handle those formidable tasks. If you are working with a design/build firm they will of course supervise the construction, but you will still want separate contracts for design and construction.

Every design contract should include certain key points. The box on page 91 discusses the items that any design contract should cover.

Most architects and designers will have a standard form contract. You are not required to use this contract as written. Many contracts lean heavily toward "protection" clauses that state what will happen if something goes wrong, but are weak in clearly stating what work will be done, who will do it, when, and for how much money. And of course, that is the real purpose of a contract. You also want the contract to protect you, but contract clauses will not prevent things from going wrong. Your best protection against problems is a clear understanding between you and the design professional of what will be done and who will do it. Your contract should define this understanding.

In all contractual matters it is best to consult an attorney. If you do not have one, find one who specializes in real estate matters and have the attorney review the document before you sign it.

The professional design process

The design phase is an evolutionary process in which you and the designer will be increasingly able to visualize an end result and make correct decisions. Here is a general outline of how a design project proceeds when the drawings are being done by a professional.

1. Analysis of existing site and structure. The first thing that happens is the development of a detailed drawing of your present house—the base plan that you drew up in Chapter 2. It identifies load-bearing walls, location of plumbing, electrical lines, and heating ducts, and any other structural items that might affect your addition plans. At this stage, the architect or designer should also inspect for underground obstructions or instabilities. If you already have blueprints or drawings of the original house, give them to the designer.

2. Review of legal restrictions. The next step is a thorough study of zoning and building permit regulations, easements, or restrictive covenants. The designer identifies any restrictions that may affect your plans.

3. General meeting. When the designer has gathered this information, you will meet to discuss the findings and to define more specifically everything you want, the kinds of materials you like, how you plan to use the new space, furnishings you will include, and any restrictions that may alter your original thoughts.

At this point the designer will probably also discuss alternative courses of action. If you have been considering a second story, the designer may suggest a new wing. Be sure that your budget limitations are clearly understood, and that what you are discussing has a reasonable chance of being achieved.

4. Selection of a basic approach. After your discussion, the designer will provide some preliminary sketches of alternative approaches. These will be basic design drawings with very little in the way of specifications. Their purpose is to define space and design features. They may also include artistic concepts of appearance, particularly for the exterior. From these approaches you should be able to choose the one that will proceed to the preliminary design and cost estimate phase.

It is important that you and the designer remain as objective as possible throughout the design process. Be willing to listen to your designer's suggestions, and be sure that he or she listens to you.

5. Preliminary design. The next phase of work may be the most critical part of your project. During this phase, the designer lays out the addition and how it will work with the existing structure in terms of traffic flow and so on, and prepares preliminary drawings in sufficient detail to get a meaningful cost estimate.

You will make final decisions on the design features you want to include, and on the exact dimensions of each

room, and you will select materials and fixtures. You will also consider tradeoffs at this point. For example, you may decide to put more money into your new kitchen and less into the new family room or guest bedroom. These kinds of decisions often make it possible to get everything you want within your budget.

6. Preliminary cost estimate. Design questions are dealt with in pieces, and only the cost estimate will reveal the sum of the parts. The preliminary cost estimate should be done by a contractor, who is generally more aware than architects and designers of actual building costs. Your architect or designer may select the contractor for this job, or you can have the estimate done by a contractor of your choice.

7. Final design. During this last phase you will adjust the budget and make decisions on all details. No major changes should be necessary after this; in fact, they should be avoided,

since they become increasingly expensive as your project matures.

This is your last chance to be sure that you are properly visualizing the final result. You should ask for drawings, sketches, or three-dimensional models, if necessary, to be sure you understand what you are approving for construction.

8. Working drawings and specifications. As discussed in the previous chapter, the final product of the design phase is the working drawings. The designer will incorporate into the working drawings and written specifications all of the information needed by the contractor or whoever does the actual construction. These extremely detailed documents include specifications for materials and fixtures, where everything is to be located, how things are to be built, elevations of vertical surfaces, precise dimensions, finish details, and all other information required for exact communication with the builder.

What a design contract should include

1. A statement that says who will review zoning and building codes and analyze the existing structure to define restrictions that may affect design, and when this will be done.

2. A clear list of the design phases, what work each phase will include, and the amount of time to be allocated to each.

3. A definition of what concept drawings, models, and other visual materials will be provided.

4. A description of how a cost estimate based on the preliminary design will be obtained. This estimate should be provided by a contractor and should be guaranteed based on the parameters defined.

5. A guarantee that the final design will meet codes and conform to zoning.

6. A description of what the specified construction documents (plans, products, and materials lists) will include. A statement that defines how

the construction documents will be approved and accepted. (A review by the actual builder is a good way to catch any problems early on.)

7. A definition of what responsibility the design professional will take during the construction phase.

8. A clear definition of payment schedules. Design professionals generally work on an hourly rate. This hourly rate can be tied to design phases with estimated time allocations for each phase. You will need to define how additional charges will accrue if these time estimates are exceeded and how changes to the design will be handled if construction estimates are too high. You can put a ceiling on total design costs by including a "not to exceed" figure. This is commonly defined as 10 to 20 percent of anticipated construction costs.

9. A clear delineation of who is responsible for what.

THE ECONOMICS OF ADDING ON

To determine whether it makes financial sense to add to your home, ask yourself: Could I sell the enlarged house for a price equal to its current market value plus the cost of the addition? Let's look at the parts of this equation.

Does adding on make economic sense?

If you're looking at homes to purchase, the current market value is obvious—it's the asking price of the home adjusted for any structural or other defects it may have. But if you've lived in your home for a number of years, you may not know exactly what its market value is. There are a couple of ways to find out.

Determining current market value

First, you can contact one or more real estate agents and ask them what they think your house might bring if you were to put it up for sale. Most will be happy to take a look at your home. Second, some professional appraisal services may be willing to provide information about recent appraisals in your neighborhood.

The key is to be sure the homes are comparable to yours in square footage, number of bedrooms and bathrooms, size of lot, age, condition, and so on. Also determine the price range in your neighborhood, and find out why homes on the high end of the scale command their higher prices. Is it a matter of their size, location, architectural style, upkeep?

Calculating add-on costs

Once you have an idea of what you want—another bathroom, a family room, more bedrooms—it's possible to come up with a ballpark figure for your addition even before you start your detailed planning.

Let's say that you're thinking about adding a master bedroom/bath combination to your two-bedroom home. The section on room-by-room planning, on pages 77–80, can help you estimate the cost. Here you'll find that the minimum size for a bedroom is about 70 square feet. Since you're thinking about a master suite, with room for a king-size bed, lots of closets, space for a desk and maybe a love seat, and a built-in cabinet for the television and stereo, you'll want to triple the figure, to 210 square feet. A 5- by 7-foot bath, the minimum recommended, adds 35 square feet to the total. Now allow some room for a double sink and perhaps a bench and increase this to 50 square feet. Your addition is now 260 square feet. Remember, all you want is a rough idea of size.

What will a 260-square-foot addition cost? An addition is new construction, so you need to find out the per-square-foot cost of new construction in your area. You can call a few contractors, watch the newspapers for articles about construction costs in your area, or ask the company that insures your home for this information—they generally call it "replacement cost." Your bank or savings and loan association might also be able to supply a figure.

Keep in mind that in a new home the cost of kitchen appliances and bathroom fixtures is averaged over the total square footage of the house. If you're planning to add a new bathroom or kitchen to an older house, the cost per square foot of your addition will be higher than the *average* new-construction cost because of the concentration of appliances or fixtures in the add-on.

Take the per-square-foot cost figure, multiply it by the square footage of your planned addition, and you have a *rough* idea of what your dream addition would cost if you hired someone else to build it.

Weighing the economics

Now add the cost of the addition to the current market value of your house and compare the total with the selling prices of homes in your neighborhood that are similar to your house with its planned addition. Is the figure in the ballpark?

An important economic rule of thumb is, don't overdo it. If the market value of your home plus the cost of the addition is more than 20 percent higher than the selling price of the best homes in your neighborhood, the economics don't look promising.

But the final decision involves more than mere dollars and cents. If you've owned your home for some time, you probably paid substantially less for it than its current market value. You've built up equity in it through both the mortgage payments you make each month and the effects of inflation on its value. If you plan to stay in your home for ten or twenty more years, you might decide that the pleasure an addition would bring you and your family more than outweighs the chance that you wouldn't recover its entire cost if you sold the house. The same reasoning doesn't make economic sense, however, if you might sell the house within the next few years or if you're shopping for a house to add on to.

Add-ons that pay off

Social trends, family size, and fashion all affect the desirability of certain home features at a given time. Few home buyers today place much value on root cellars or servants' quarters, although there were times when many homeowners considered each of these essential. The basement recreation room popular in the 1950s and 1960s has given way to a space more in tune with today's life-styles: the family room with plenty of light and proximity to the kitchen.

Certain features seem to retain their attractiveness over time, however. Despite smaller families, most buyers still prefer three-bedroom homes, so adding an extra bedroom to a two-bedroom house can make good economic sense. A fourth bedroom may not increase the salability of a house as much, although the demand for home offices is strong in families where both spouses work. If a home has only one bathroom, addition of a second bath also will generally pay off. And a modern, roomy kitchen with up-to-date appliances boosts a home's sales appeal as long as the kitchen is not overdone.

Greenhouse and sunspace additions are currently in fashion and may continue to be so over the long run because of the energy benefits they can offer.

Bear in mind, however, that structural repairs or improvements—replacing a roof, repairing a shaky foundation—add little or no value to a home. (Failure to attend to maintenance will, however, reduce a home's worth.) Keep in mind also that part of the cost of adding on may be for structural repairs or alterations to the original house.

Ultimately, of course, considerations other than economics will play a part in your decision. This is your house—the place where you spend much of your leisure time. You'll probably decide to make it as pleasant and efficient as you can afford to.

Can you afford your dream addition?

Adding on to a house generally involves a significant financial commitment. To see if your dream can become a reality, you need to assess your personal financial picture: your net worth and monthly cash flow. Getting all the figures together at the outset will encourage you to plan realistically, and it will simplify the loan application process if you decide to finance your addition.

Financing your addition

Now that you've pinned down exactly what your addition will look like and have some idea of how much it will cost, the final step is to arrange for the money to build it.

The three basic options are using savings, converting investments or other assets to cash, and borrowing. If all these options are open to you, you may wish to consult your financial advisor for help in deciding among them. Among the factors you'll need to take into account are the return you would forgo on savings or investments if you used them to pay for the addition; whether dipping into savings would reduce your financial safety cushion below what is prudent; and the tax advantages borrowing provides versus its cost.

Choosing a loan

This section outlines the loan options available to homeowners who decide to borrow the funds for an addition.

Personal loans. If you'll need $5,000 or less to complete your addition, a personal loan can provide the funds. Also called credit card loans or line of credit loans, they generally carry much higher rates of interest and have shorter payback periods than loans secured by real estate. However, you can borrow smaller amounts than from a mortgage lender, and you may be able to draw funds only as you need them.

Private party loans—those arranged between individuals—are another type of personal loan. If you have a relative or a friend who is willing to lend you money, this can be an excellent way to finance an addition. Since the parties to the loan set both the terms and the interest rate, this route can offer the lender a better return than he or she is now getting in the marketplace while at the same time providing the borrower with a lower interest rate than might be available through conventional sources.

Insurance or investment loans. Another way to finance a home addition is to borrow against the cash value of your life insurance policy or against the market value of stocks or bonds. (You can generally borrow up to 80 percent of the market value of

securities.) Because your policy or investments act as collateral, these loans are generally easy to get; and loans against insurance policies may carry favorable rates of interest and payback terms. Keep in mind, though, that borrowing against insurance reduces the amount beneficiaries would receive should anything happen to the insured during the term of the loan. And if the market value of your securities should fall, the lender could ask for immediate repayment of a portion of the loan.

Home equity loans. Although terminology differs among lenders, home equity loans, home improvement loans, and second mortgages are basically similar. The collateral for these loans is the *equity* (the difference between what your home is worth and what you owe on it) that you have built up in your home. They usually carry lower rates and longer repayment periods (5 to 15 years, depending on the size of the loan) than personal loans, but higher rates and shorter terms than regular mortgage loans.

The Federal Housing Administration (FHA) and the Veterans Administration (VA) back some loans of this type, which carry a slightly lower interest rate than do those through conventional sources. However, funding for such loans is limited, and processing times can be lengthy.

The U.S. Department of Housing and Urban Development (HUD) also backs low-interest loans, which are offered through local housing authorities. These loans are available to residents of targeted urban areas, who must also qualify on the basis of income. Check with your local housing authority if you believe your neighborhood might be included in this program.

Refinancing your mortgage. If you'll need at least $20,000 to pay for your addition, it may pay to refinance the mortgage on your home—and at the same time increase its size.

If your home is now worth $75,000, for example, and you owe $30,000 on your original mortgage, the lender that holds that mortgage—or another lender—should be willing to issue a new mortgage for at least 80 percent of the current value of your house, or $60,000. After paying off the $30,000 on the original mortgage, you would have $30,000 (less the costs of refinancing) to pay for your addition. Of course, you would also be facing higher monthly mortgage payments on a $60,000 loan.

Here are some of the positive points about refinancing:
☐ You'll be able to spread the payments for your addition over the term of the new mortgage—at least 15 years, and often 30.
☐ You'll make one payment a month rather than two.

Here are some of the negatives:
☐ You may have to exchange a low-interest-rate mortgage for one at a substantially higher rate.
☐ You will have to pay closing costs (which can amount to 4 or 5 percent of the loan) and points (1 point equals 1 percent of the loan amount) on the new mortgage, and you may incur a prepayment penalty (perhaps equal to 6 months' interest) to retire your old mortgage early.

To help you decide whether it makes better sense to refinance your mortgage or to take out a separate loan to pay for an addition, call some lenders to determine their current interest rates and repayment terms and then calculate the costs under each scenario. The monthly loan payment table at right will give you the information you'll need.

First calculate the monthly payment for a second mortgage at, say, 14 percent over 10 years and add that to your current monthly payment. Compare that figure with the monthly payment on a larger mortgage at the current interest rate over a 30-year or other term. Then take into account refinancing costs (closing costs, points). Also calculate the tax benefits (higher interest deductions) that a refinanced mortgage will provide and compare them with the tax benefits of your current mortgage plus the second mortgage. Finally,

Calculating monthly loan payments

Find the interest rate and term of the loan you're considering. Multiply the factor given in the table times the number of thousands in the loan to determine the monthly payment. For example, monthly payments on a $50,000 mortgage at 10.5 percent for a 30-year term would be about $457: 9.147 x 50 = $457.35

Annual interest rate	5	Factor per $1,000 Term of loan (years) 10	15	30
9.0	20.758	12.668	10.143	8.046
9.5	21.102	12.940	10.442	8.409
10.0	21.247	13.215	10.746	8.776
10.5	21.494	13.494	11.054	9.147
11.0	21.742	13.775	11.366	9.523
11.5	21.993	14.060	11.682	9.903
12.0	22.244	14.347	12.002	10.286
12.5	22.498	14.638	12.325	10.673
13.0	22.753	14.931	12.652	11.062
13.5	23.010	15.227	12.983	11.454
14.0	23.268	15.527	13.317	11.849
15.0	23.790	16.134	13.996	12.644
16.0	24.318	16.751	14.687	13.448

remember that many fees included in closing costs will be the same no matter what the size of the mortgage; therefore, closing costs weigh more heavily the smaller the size of the refinanced mortgage.

Here's a rule of thumb regarding refinancing in general: If the interest rate of the new mortgage is 2 percentage points lower than that of the present mortgage, and if you plan to own your home for three to five years longer, refinancing the outstanding mortgage (without adding to its size) should pay off.

When you shop for a new mortgage, you'll find a variety of choices: fixed-rate loans, adjustable-rate mortgages (ARMs) with various indexes for determining when and how much the rate will change, and graduated-payment ARMs with lower initial payments but potential for negative amortization. You may be able to choose terms ranging from 15 to 30 years.

If you're considering refinancing, it's essential to do some informed shopping among lenders. Banks, savings and loans, and mortgage brokers are the three common sources of mortgage money. A bank or savings and loan may offer 25 or 30 different loan options, while a mortgage broker may have as many as 10,000

options. Check the number of points each lender will charge to grant the loan; lenders offering the lowest interest rates sometimes make up for this with higher points. And if you're considering an ARM, determine whether it has a cap (a ceiling on how much the interest rate can rise) and calculate how high payments could go in a high-inflation economy.

Applying for your loan

Establishing your creditworthiness is a matter of showing the ability to pay back the money you are borrowing and having sufficient collateral to ensure repayment should something unforeseen happen. Each lender has its own criteria, but having all your financial information in hand should simplify the process.

When it's time for the final loan application, you will probably need your final drawings in hand, and you may need a few hundred dollars in application fees. Some loans—personal or those against insurance or securities—may be had within a day or two of your application. Loans that use your real estate as collateral can take anywhere from one to six weeks in processing.

INDEX